ANXIETY TOOLKIT FOR TEENS

Anxiety Healing, Reducing Stress, Panic Attacks, and Controlling Emotions for Teens, to Make Them Strong and Internally Healthy.

By

Kangaroo Publications

© **Copyright 2022 by Kangaroo Publications - All rights reserved.**

Without the prior written permission of the Publisher, no part of this publication may be stored in a retrieval system, replicated, or transferred in any form or medium, digital, scanning, recording, printing, mechanical, or otherwise, except as permitted under 1976 United States Copyright Act, section 107 or 108. Permission concerns should be directed to the publisher's permission department.

Legal Notice

This book is copyright protected. It is only to be used for personal purposes. Without the author's or publisher's permission, you cannot paraphrase, quote, copy, distribute, sell, or change any part of the information in this book.

Disclaimer Notice

This book is written and published independently. Please keep in mind that the material in this publication is solely for educational and entertaining purposes. All efforts have provided authentic, up-to-date, trustworthy, and comprehensive information. There are no express or implied assurances. The purpose of this book's material is to assist readers in having a better understanding of the subject matter. The activities, information, and exercises are provided solely for self-help information. This book is not intended to replace expert psychologists, legal, financial, or other guidance. If you require counseling, please get in touch with a qualified professional.

By reading this text, the reader accepts that the author will not be held liable for any damages, indirectly or directly, experienced due to the use of the information included herein, particularly, but not limited to, omissions, errors, or inaccuracies. As a reader, you are accountable for your decisions, actions, and consequences.

CONTENTS

INTRODUCTION 6
WHAT ARE TEENAGERS ANXIOUS ABOUT? 8
CHAPTER 1: ANXIETY IN TEENS IS RISING: WHAT'S GOING ON? 9
   1.1 How Did We Get Here? 9
   1.2 Real Problem is the Rise in Anxiety 10
   1.3 Be Aware of the Signs of Anxiety 10
   1.4 Anxiety and Other Mental Health Issues 11
CHAPTER 2: WHEN IS ANXIETY A PROBLEM? 15
   2.1 When Is Anxiety Normal? 16
   2.2 Anxious Feelings Can Be Uncomfortable 17
   2.3 Know Anxiety Is Treatable! 17
   2.4 Helping Teenagers Manage Anxious Feelings 18
   2.5 Activities and Worksheets to Manage Anxiety 20
      My Anxiety Levels 21
      Anxiety Breakdown 22
      Anxiety vs. Truth 23
      Negative Thoughts 24
      Changing my Thoughts 25
      Automatic Negative Thoughts 26
      If I Change 27
      I Can Cope 28
CHAPTER 3: TEENS OVERLOADED WITH STRESS: WHEN THIS HAPPENS? 29
   3.1 Signs of Too Much Stress 29
   3.2 How Does Stress Work? 30
   3.3 Stress Management and Teens 31

3.4 Activities and Worksheets to Manage Stress 33
    How Am I Feeling 34
    Things That Causes Me Stress 35
    Stress Management Reflection 36
    Dealing with My Worries 37
    Anger Thermometer 38
    When I Feel Angry 39
    My Stress Journal 40

CHAPTER 4: PANIC ATTACK: A FRIGHTENING EXPERIENCE 41
4.1 Symptoms of a Panic Attack 42
4.2 Causes of Panic in Teens 43
4.3 Helping Teens with Panic Disorder 44
4.4 Activities and Worksheets to Control Panic Attacks .. 45
    My Panic Symptoms 46
    Panic Assessment 48
    My Subconscious Expectations 49
    Problem Solving 50
    I am Someone Who 51

CHAPTER 5: LIVING HEALTHILY: EXPRESS THE EMOTIONS YOU FEEL 52
5.1 Learning to React Well 52
5.2 What Would You Do? 54
5.3 Handle The Roller Coaster of Emotions 55
5.4 Activities and Worksheets to Control Emotions 59
    Feelings and Emotions 59
    Emotions Worksheet 60
    Getting to Know My Emotions 61
    How Are You Feeling Today? 62

When I Feel Sad 63
When I Felt... 64
All Feelings Are Okay 65
Coping with Feelings 67
5.5 Meditation and Mindfulness Activities 69
Let it Go 74
Forgiveness Fingers 75
Gratitude Journal 76
Self-Awareness Happiness Assessment 77
My Learning Sheet 78
About My Day 79
Growth Mindset 80
Rainbow Breathing 81
Lazy 8 Breathing 82
Beach Day Breath 83
Dragon Breathing 84
Yoga Poses 85
HOW CAN PARENTS HELP? 86
THE END NOTE 98

INTRODUCTION

Anxiety is the sensation that something unpleasant is about to happen or that you won't be able to handle a scenario. The sensation is accompanied by physical symptoms like "butterflies in the stomach," stress, trembling, nausea, and perspiration. These behaviors include trying to avoid the source of the fear or seeking a lot of comfort.

Anxiety is the feeling you experience as you become tense when your heart starts to beat quickly, when your breathing becomes a little rapid, and when you're concerned about something. It's common to experience some worry occasionally, especially for teenagers. It can support motivation for the job, education, or sports and assist in keeping them safe. However, if these uneasy sensations persist, they may make it difficult to focus in class, interact with friends, or simply enjoy life.

Anxiety can arise in response to a particular circumstance or event but can also persist after it has passed. It is also possible for it to occur in the absence of a certain circumstance or occurrence. But it's normal to feel anxious. Everyone has occasional anxiety.

Stress and anxiety can both appear and feel similar. Stress is a reaction to pressures, obstacles, or events from the outside world. Your child's heart rate may increase, respiration may quicken, and muscles may tense up under stress. Understanding the distinction between stress and anxiety will help you better understand how your child is feeling and how to support them.

In the years leading up to adolescence, anxiety is highly prevalent. This is due to the emotional, physical, and social changes that occur during adolescence, which also coincide with the maturation of adolescent brains. Teenagers and preteens want greater freedom and fresh experiences. Teenagers naturally experience anxiety in response to these chances, challenges, and changes.

Pre-teens and teenagers, for instance, could have anxiety before starting secondary school, dressing a certain way, fitting in with friends, beginning their first job, participating in school plays, or attending formal events. Additionally, when their independence grows, they could experience anxiety related to obligations, finances, and jobs.

Teenagers' and preteens' anxiety isn't always a bad thing. Teenagers can be safe by being anxious since it makes them consider their surroundings. It may also inspire them to exert their best effort. Additionally, it can assist students in preparing for difficult circumstances like public speaking or athletic competitions. Anxiety can affect a teen's life in different ways. Anxiety Toolkit for Teens will guide you and your teens about anxiety and other disorders linked with it.

WHAT ARE TEENAGERS ANXIOUS ABOUT?

There are some things that teenagers could be anxious about;

Their Performance: We find a lot of worry of not performing well. Beyond a high work ethic, a lot of anxiety is focused toward perfectionism, or the drive to achieve their utmost best in school. Teenagers claim they experience enormous pressure to perform well even if their parents advise them not to worry about college admissions.

How people view them. Every adolescent is going to have a consciousness of and a certain vigilance about how they're being regarded. The outcome may be crippling social anxiety. They're going to be thinking way too much about whether they might come across as foolish or inept, or they're worrying way too much about doing something embarrassing.

Their body parts. Many youngsters find the physical changes of puberty to be uncomfortable. Children may feel strange and out of place if they develop either earlier than most of their peers or later than them. For girls, being on the early side of the development will have a more detrimental effect than being on time or even late with development. Boys are particularly sensitive to height. The influence on a 16-year-self-esteem and confidence can be significant if they haven't reached puberty and appear to be 13 years old while their peers appear to be 20 years old. Body dysmorphic disorder is a severe form of anxiety that some children experience. They become so fixated on a genuine or perceived physical imperfection that it severely impairs their functioning.

CHAPTER 1

ANXIETY IN TEENS IS RISING: WHAT'S GOING ON?

About one in every three teenagers between the ages of 14 and 19 will have an anxiety disorder, based on the National Institute of Mental Health. These numbers have been rising steadily; between 2006 and 2013, there was a 23% rise in the number of anxiety disorders in children and adolescents. These numbers, along with the fact that the number of hospital admissions for suicidal young people has increased in the last ten years, have generated a lot of worrisome questions.

1.1 How Did We Get Here?

What is happening?

Various things could be the cause, though are unsure. Consider the following factors in addition to genetics, brain chemistry, personality, and life events:

<u>High standards and pressure to perform well.</u> As we discussed earlier, today's youth may experience pressure to perform in ways past generations did not because of standardized testing and a mindset of achievement. In a yearly poll conducted by Higher Education Research, first-year college students are asked if they feel overburdened by everything they need to do. Compared to 29% in 2001 and 17% in 1986, 43% of students responded "yes" in 2017.

<u>A dangerous and unsettling world</u>. As a result of the rise in school shootings, vacation drills have been implemented in schools. Public shootings have occurred. There have been numerous fatal terrorist attacks abroad and in the United States.

It is understandable for anyone to experience fear in public areas that previously felt safe simply by watching or reading the news.

The internet. Children and teenagers of today are continuously logged into social media. It is not unexpected that replies to social media posts influence how they feel about themselves and how they view the world. They find it difficult to resist comparing their lives and social relationships to what they see on social media.

Additionally, some kids worry excessively about day-to-day activities like going to school, a party, having a sleepover, or going to camp, which is an unanticipated and disproportionate response to a child's regular experiential learning. Frequently, this begins in the years just before puberty.

1.2 Real Problem is the Rise in Anxiety

Depression, substance abuse, and even suicide are major mental health issues caused by chronic anxiety. It might make it difficult to concentrate and study, which can lead to issues in school that may last a lifetime. Physical issues like headaches, persistent pain, digestive issues, and later heart disease can also result from it.

All socioeconomic groups suburban, urban, and rural are affected by anxiety disorders. Both those who are and are not headed for college are impacted.

1.3 Be Aware of the Signs of Anxiety

Children occasionally express their anxiety verbally, but other times it is less obvious especially since they might not even be aware of it. Recurrent concerns and worries about mundane aspects of daily life are among the warning signs.

- o Alterations in behavior, including irritability
- o Avoiding social interactions, activities, or school
- o Declining grades or skipping classes
- o Difficulty sleeping or focusing
- o Alcoholism, drug use, or other dangerous behaviors

- Bodily symptoms frequently recur, such as exhaustion, headaches, or stomachaches.

Discuss potential sources of stress with the kids. Try to view the world from their perspective and assist them in maintaining perspective and coping mechanisms.

Be careful with the standards you set for kids and teenagers. Children can achieve their potential with high expectations, but these expectations must be reasonable. Additionally, remember that kids require downtime to unwind, play, and spend time with friends all of which are essential for their mental and physical well-being. And we must keep in mind that life is about more than just success.

Children's use of social media should be discussed. Encourage them to take breaks and reflect critically and logically on how social media affects their lives.

1.4 Anxiety and Other Mental Health Issues

Teenagers are skilled at hiding their emotions; thus, anxiety is frequently disregarded. But these are some of the actions that might indicate anxiety in a teen.

- Persistent phobias and concerns regarding everyday occurrences
- Irritability
- Difficulty concentrating
- Excessive sensitivity to criticism or self-consciousness
- Absence from social activities avoidance of challenging or novel situations
- Persistent symptoms of headaches or stomachaches
- Declining grades or leaving school
- Repeatedly looking for assurance
- Issues with sleep
- Use of drugs
- Anxiety and skipping school

School can be the backdrop for many things a teen may be nervous about because so much of what adolescents are focused on is associated with school - think academics, sports, other activities, and social life. Therefore, it's not always about the school when kids object to attending school.

School phobia, which means that the cause of the person's worry is the school has been identified by a psychologist. According to him, instead, dealing with kids who frequently make reasons to remain home or outright refuse to attend some event puts less emphasis on their choice to skip school. We're more interested in their motivation for not attending school.

"Worrying over being called upon by a teacher randomly and messing up or experiencing a mental attack in class or worry that others would make fun of them because they don't look right could be the issue...," psychologist continues, "you could interview a hundred youngsters refusing to go to school and get a hundred different reasons."

- o **Using Drugs and Feeling Anxious**

Like adults, anxious teenagers may turn to recreational drugs, especially marijuana, to ease their pain. According to psychologist, it is self-medication, and the truth is that it is effective in the short run. It does reduce stress and anxiety. It dulls it. It does turn off your brain's worry center. However, because the worry endures and the kid develops a dependency on the substance, it is a bad coping strategy over time.

Teenagers frequently tell him that marijuana is healthier than alcohol, according to psychologist. Aside from that, it's now simpler than ever to smoke - on the street, at home, or school because marijuana is legal in many regions (for those over 21), and vaping is possible.

He cautions youth against using recreational substances as medicine, noting that neither is a healthy method to manage anxiety. "Having a bottle of vodka in your desk drawer at work is no different from carrying around a joint in your pocket all day to get through the school day," the psychologist said. You're still depending on a chemical to get by each day, and the more you use it, the more reliant you'll get on it.

- **Concern and Sadness**

Teenagers frequently exhibit symptoms of both depression and anxiety. That is partly because living with anxiety can be so upsetting or restricting that it triggers depression.

Psychologist recalls helping a young person who experienced severe social anxiety after transferring to a new high school. She started to avoid activities because she feared failing in a more competitive setting. She later experienced a panic attack and started to isolate herself from her friends out of fear that she might do so in front of them. She eventually got so lonely that she suffered from serious depression.

According to him, this type of anxiety and depression layering is typical and frequently overlooked. A doctor won't succeed if they only address the anxiety while ignoring the depression's presenting symptoms.

However, it's also plausible that depression and anxiety are two distinct co-occurring disorders.

Psychologist explains: "The question I ask them is: Would you still be depressed if I could just enter your brain and remove your anxiety?" It might be a case of co-occurring depression if they responded, "Yes, I would still be depressed." I would assume that the anxiety is what's creating the sadness if the response is, "No, I would feel fantastic if you took the anxiety away."

Generalized anxiety disorder, or GAD as it is usually known, is strongly associated with depression later in life, according to psychologist, to the point where it is also regarded as a precursor to depression. GAD is anxiety brought on by excessive and persistent worry over a wide range of everyday concerns rather than by a specific thing (known as a specific phobia).

What ties anxiety and depression together?

According to psychologist, anxiety impairs well-being. You are more at risk for depression if you lack confidence in your ability to make wise decisions and if you live defensively.

If everything in life is a "what if?" and you go through life worried and doubting constantly, that will significantly impact how you view yourself, your confidence, and your self-esteem, he says. He continues by saying that it is not surprising that living defensively and on a constant diet of dread could result in sadness.

CHAPTER 2

WHEN IS ANXIETY A PROBLEM?

Teenagers with anxiety differ from children with anxiety. Children worry more about things like the gloom, monsters, or anything horrible occurring to their parents when they are younger. Teenagers, however, are more inclined to worry about themselves.

This frequently appears as perfectionism. Teenagers may worry about performing poorly in sports or school. Alternatively, they might be too concerned with what other people think of them. Children frequently worry about their bodies, too. A significant trigger is experiencing puberty sooner or after their friends.

While some worried teenagers have long struggled, things have gotten worse. In other instances, children who previously had no anxiety suddenly develop it as they get older. Two types of anxiety, panic episodes and social anxiety, frequently begin in adolescence.

Teenagers are skilled at masking their emotions, so it can be challenging to detect anxiousness. The symptoms also differ from child to child. Some adolescent people choose to stay away from things. Others become angrier or snap at those around them. They can begin skipping class or make frequent complaints about aches and stomach pains.

Teens who experience anxiety may develop a habit of using alcohol or drugs to relax. In the short term, it functions. However, their fear doesn't go away, and kids may develop a dependency on the drug over time. It is common for anxiety to trigger depression. Living in fear or avoidance negatively impacts well-being. Very nervous kids get depressed as they begin to do less and less.

Cognitive behavioral therapy is the most effective treatment for adolescents with anxiety (CBT). CBT teaches children how to confront their anxiety rather than running from it. Then they discover that their anxiety does lessen with time. For children who are too apprehensive about completing CBT alone, antidepressant medication may occasionally be added to CBT.

2.1 When Is Anxiety Normal?

It is common to experience anxiety, jitters, or worry occasionally. You may have experienced anxiety when you are required to speak in front of a group or anxious before a large test or a tryout. Perhaps you have experienced anxiety when unsure of the safety of your surroundings or in case of a loved one's sickness.

A lot of people have experienced this.

Although painful, anxious sensations have a purpose. They forewarn you that something important to you is at risk. You can feel apprehensive and think, "I need to perform well here." Alternatively, "This counts — get ready." Or; "Be cautious".

The body's fight-or-flight reaction is triggered by anxiety. Thanks to a normal hormonal release, you can gather the attention and energy you need for a task or potential threat. The fight-or-flight reaction is what triggers the physical symptoms of anxiety.

For instance, you might get "butterflies" in your stomach when you're anxious. You can also have clammy hands or sweaty palms. You might feel a little dryness in your mouth. Or you notice a slight warmth on your face. Your breathing or heartbeat may feel accelerated. You may experience one or more of these symptoms when you are anxious.

Feelings like these can motivate you to take the necessary action. Even if you're anxious, you can still attempt the test or try out. To ensure your safety, you can look at yourself. Instead of getting sucked into the concern, you can concentrate on what a loved one needs and make plans for how to assist.

When you understand that your level of worry is appropriate for the circumstance, you can stop giving your worried thoughts and feelings your undivided attention. You can focus on what has to be done in its place. You don't have to take action to get your anxiousness to "go away." You can take a deep breath and take on the difficulty. Anxiety will eventually go away on its own.

2.2 Anxious Feelings Can Be Uncomfortable

Some people experience excessive levels of anxiety. It appears to be more than they can handle. They spend too much time and energy on their concerns or fears. Some people may start avoiding situations or persons who make them uneasy. These behaviors may indicate an anxiety problem.

Inform your parents, the school counselor, or the doctor if you believe your anxiety is out of control. Disorders of anxiety can be treated. The quicker you begin receiving assistance, the better you'll feel.

2.3 Know Anxiety Is Treatable!

80% of children with a diagnosable anxiety disorder do not receive treatment, even though anxiety disorders are quite curable. The earlier a problem is diagnosed, as with most issues, the simpler it is to treat.

Cognitive behavioral therapy (CBT) is the most effective therapies for anxiety disorders. The main goals of CBT are to help the child think differently about his fears, expose him to more of his feared circumstances, and employ relaxation techniques, including breathing exercises, relaxation techniques, and encouraging self-talk. Increased exposure to feared things or activities is the main goal of exposure therapy, a form of cognitive behavioral therapy.

According to studies, 80% of children with anxiety disorders respond favorably to a 12-week course of CBT combined with medication. 66% of those kids showed no or little signs of anxiousness after the 12-week treatment. 65% of the children receiving CBT alone responded favorably, with roughly 37% of those kids exhibiting no or minor anxiety symptoms. It's crucial to remember that drugs can be given safely and are a crucial component of treating children's anxiety disorders.

As with any mental health condition, regular sleep, exercise, meditation, relaxation techniques, and yoga are all vital components in treating anxiety disorders. These, however, are not a replacement for CBT or medicine. The most crucial thing is to be conscious of your kids' mental health, to inquire about it, and to request assistance.

2.4 Helping Teenagers Manage Anxious Feelings

You can assist your child in developing this crucial life skill by teaching them how to regulate their anxiety. Here are some suggestions.

- **Encourage your kid to express their fears.**

You can help your child feel less worried by just talking to them about the things that worry them. You can better comprehend what's happening with your child by talking to them and listening. And when you comprehend, you're better prepared to assist your child in controlling their anxiety or locating solutions to issues.

- **Recognize your child's emotions**

Your child's fear is real, even if the event they are afraid of is unlikely to occur. This implies that it's crucial to notice your child's fear and reassure them that they can manage it. Instead of encouraging them not to worry, do this since telling a youngster not to worry implies that fear is an invalid emotion. For instance, your youngster may be worried about passing a test. Tell them you recognize their emotions and that the most important thing is that they will give their best effort.

Your child will learn to practice self-compassion in trying circumstances if you warmly and compassionately address their sentiments.

- ○ **Encourage courageous conduct**

To do this, gently encourage your child to make little goals for the things that make them feel uncomfortable. Don't pressure your kids into circumstances they don't feel prepared to handle. Your youngster may, for instance, have anxiety when performing in front of people. You can recommend that your child practice their lines in front of the family as a first step. Additionally, you can assist your kid by encouraging them to use the constructive self-talk, such as

- "I can handle this. I've had circumstances similar to this before".
- It's OK if I do this differently than others; it is an example of self-compassion.
- Being aggressive, for instance, saying, "I need some help with this assignment."

It's also beneficial to give your youngster appreciation for taking a risk, no matter how minor.

- ○ **Fostering safety and security in teenagers**

Teenagers are better able to handle puberty's daily struggles and worries when they feel safe and secure. Your actions can promote your child's sense of security by:

- Spending time with your child, such as cooking, walking, or watching a movie.
- Having a family schedule that allows for family meals and other traditions
- Allows time in your daily schedule for activities that your child finds calming, such as reading, taking walks, listening to music

- Spending time with others your child likes, trusts, and feels at ease with.
- Teenagers who adopt a healthy lifestyle can frequently manage their anxiety. For instance, taking your child for a stroll rather than letting them sit at home and worry can help to relax them.

Here are some wholesome options that can assist your kid with regular anxiety:

- Get enough exercise, proper sleep, and wholesome food and drink.
- Avoid using alcohol, caffeine, and other drugs.
- Avoid unneeded tension by not delaying or being late.
- Practice deep breathing, relaxation of the muscles, or mindfulness.

2.5 Activities and Worksheets to Manage Anxiety

Below are some activities and exercises to manage anxiety.

My Anxiety Levels

My Anxiety Levels

Use this worksheet to explore what happens to your body, thoughts and feelings as your anxiety increases! Write down the helpful coping skills that you use for each level of anxiety.

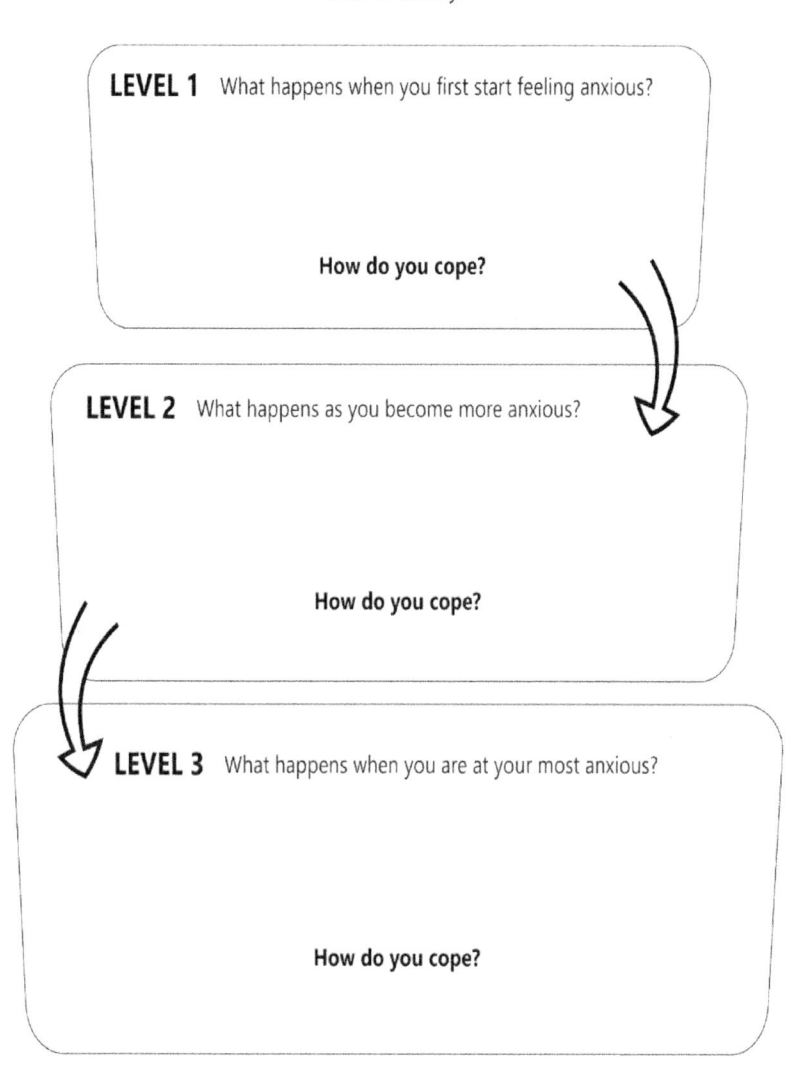

LEVEL 1 What happens when you first start feeling anxious?

How do you cope?

LEVEL 2 What happens as you become more anxious?

How do you cope?

LEVEL 3 What happens when you are at your most anxious?

How do you cope?

Anxiety Breakdown

Anxiety Breakdown

What is making me feel anxious?
_____

What are some of the negative thoughts that I am having?

How is my body responding?
_____
_____

What is the worst things that can happen?
_____

What do I have in my control to keep this from happening?
_____
_____

What are positive thoughts to help calm my mind?
_____

What are positive thoughts to help calm my mind?

Anxiety vs. Truth

Anxiety vs. Truth!

Whenever you experience anxiety your mind might begin racing with thoughts that aren't always true. Anxious thoughts focus on the worst possible outcome. These thoughts can make you believe that things are worse than they actually are and that you are not capable of coping. On the left, write a few anxious thoughts that you are experiencing then try to challenge those thoughts by identifying what is actually true about your situation.

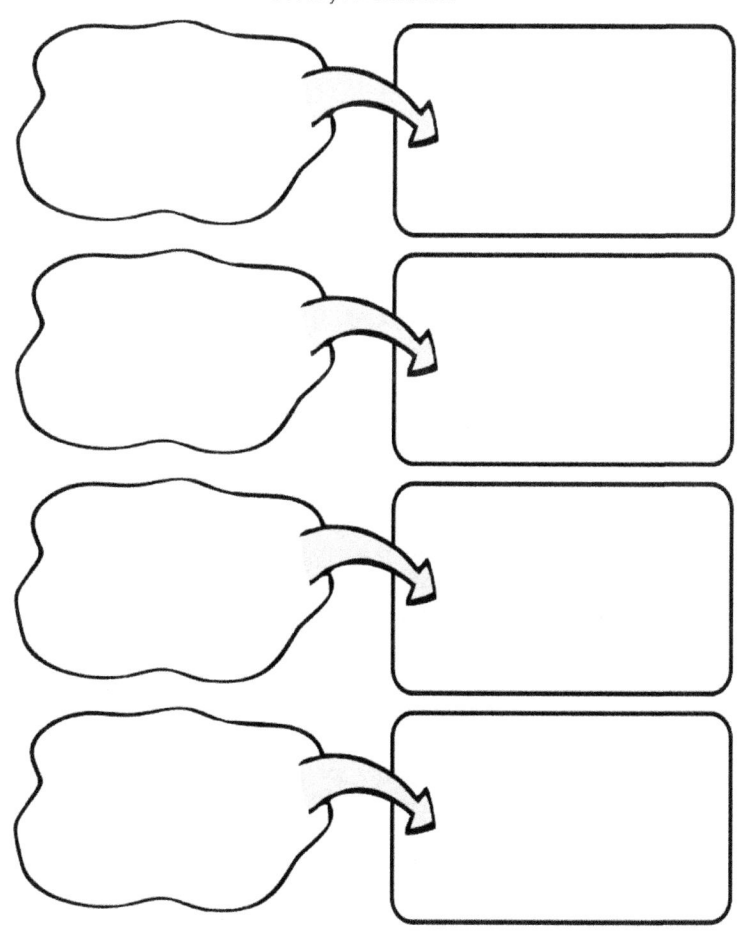

Negative Thoughts

Negative Thoughts

It is John's first day at his new school. He is having negative thoughts that are making him feel anxious. Can you help him change his thoughts?

I don't have any friends here. No one is going to like me!

My friends at my old school are having fun without me.

I'm so nervous! The kids will probably think that I'm weird.

This school is SO big. I know for sure that I'm going to get lost!

Changing My Thoughts

This is what I have been thinking

This is how I feel

So I need to think

This is how I want to feel

Automatic Negative Thoughts

Automatic Negative Thoughts

Automatic negative thoughts are thoughts that show up right away that make us feel anxious or sad. These thoughts are unhelpful and often make us feel worse about the situation. The best way to get rid of these is to challenge them and come up with new, positive thoughts!

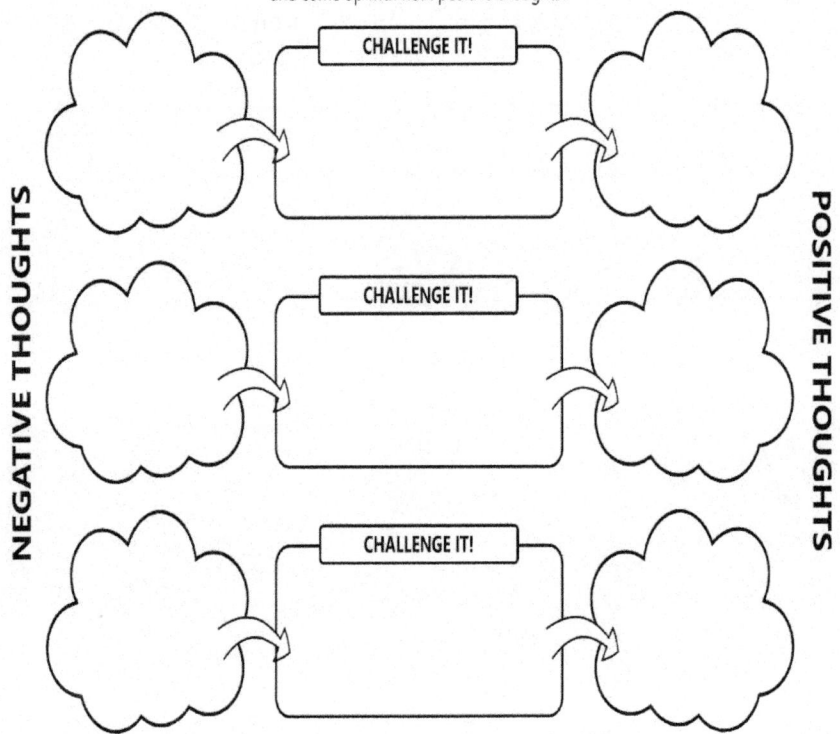

NEGATIVE THOUGHTS

CHALLENGE IT!

CHALLENGE IT!

CHALLENGE IT!

POSITIVE THOUGHTS

If I Change

If I Change.....

Use this worksheet to think about the 'pros' and 'cons' of either making a change or keeping things the same.

If I DO make a change....

PROS

CONS

If I DON'T make a change....

PROS

CONS

I Can Cope

I Can Cope! with feeling ANXIOUS

Some things that make me feel anxious are......

1. _____

2. _____

3. _____

These changes happen when I feel anxious:

Changes in my body...	Thoughts I have...	Things I do...

When I feel anxious, I can cope by:

Check all of the coping skills that might be helpful! Use the blank spaces to write in your own

- [ ] Deep breathing
- [ ] Using positive self-talk
- [ ] Meditating or relaxing
- [ ] Talking to a friend
- [ ] Talking to an adult
- [ ] Playing a game

- [ ] Going to walk
- [ ] Writing in my journal
- [ ] Practicing mindfulness
- [ ] Thinking happy thoughts
- [ ] Keeping myself busy
- [ ] Exercising

_____
_____
_____
_____
_____
_____

CHAPTER 3

TEENS OVERLOADED WITH STRESS: WHEN DOES THIS HAPPEN?

Teenagers can benefit from understanding stress management techniques because they, like adults, might encounter stress daily. Most teens become more stressed when they believe a situation to be risky, challenging, or painful and lack the tools to deal with it. Among the stressors that teens may experience are:

- Issues with peers or friends at school
- Unsafe neighborhood or living conditions
- Expectations from school and frustrations
- Loss of a close relative
- Changing locations or schools
- Alterations to their physique
- Divorce or separation of the parents
- Negative feelings or ideas about oneself
- Taking on excessive amounts of work or setting unreasonably high standards
- Family's financial situation
- Chronic disease or significant issues within the family

Some teenagers experience stress overload. This can result in physical sickness, anger, anxiety, withdrawal, or bad coping mechanisms, including drug and alcohol usage.

3.1 Signs of Too Much Stress

Youth stress symptoms can manifest in a variety of ways, including:

Children frequently struggle to express their emotions in words, and stress can occasionally boil over into irritability and rage.

Children and teenagers who are stressed out may be more irritable or argumentative than usual.

<u>*Behavior shifts*</u>: A young child who was before a terrific listener is now acting out. A formerly active teen is reluctant to leave the house today. Unexpected changes may indicate high levels of stress. A child or adolescent with problems sleeping may complain of being constantly exhausted, sleeping more than normal, or having trouble falling asleep at night.

<u>*Neglecting obligations*</u>: If a teenager starts procrastinating more than usual, forgets assignments, or suddenly falls behind on other commitments, stress may be to blame.

<u>*Changes in eating patterns*</u>: Stress can cause people to eat excessively or insufficiently. Getting sick more frequently: Physical symptoms of stress are common. Frequently stressed children complain of headaches or stomachaches and may visit the school nurse's office frequently.

3.2 How Does Stress Work?

Stress is a typical reaction to life's pressures, demands, and difficulties. It serves as a mental and physical cue to help you prepare for what lies ahead. When your brain senses a danger to your safety, your body immediately releases a wave of stress hormones. You consequently become more attentive. You widen your eyes. Your breathing and heartbeat quicken. Your heart pumps more oxygen to the muscles for increased strength and speed.

The stress response in your body serves to keep you safe. It enables you to respond immediately, fight fiercely, or flee rapidly if necessary. Stress is also referred to as the fight-or-flight reaction for this reason.

- **Regular Stress**

The majority of the time, stress-inducing factors are not harmful. Commonplace events like taking a test, being called upon in class, uncomfortable circumstances, or having too much to do frequently lead to stress. They lead to emotional stress. However, your body produces stress hormones in response to emotional stress, just like it does in response to a threat to your safety.

Because of this, you could get "butterflies" in your stomach when under emotional stress. Your breathing may feel shallow, or your heart may be beating more quickly. Perhaps you're shaking or perspiring. You should maybe pace. You might experience agitation, tension, or anxiety.

You won't need to fight or run quickly in these circumstances. You may still concentrate, gather your strength, and confront the issue with courage with the aid of your body's stress response. You begin to experience stress alleviation as soon as you take control of the issue. Your body's stress chemicals subside. The "butterfly" emotions disappear. Your heartbeat slows to a regular rate. Your entire body begins to return to a relaxed condition. You can speed up this process when you study and put stress management techniques into practice.

o **What Happens If Stress Gets Out of Hand?**

Daily tension typically results from obstacles you can overcome and cope with. However, if your stress feels overwhelming, occurs frequently, or is more than you can handle, go to a trusted adult for support and assistance.

3.3 Stress Management and Teens

Stressors are a part of life for both adults and children. These techniques can aid in managing stress:

Become more mindful. Researchers found that youths who acquired mindfulness showed noticeably less emotional anguish than teens who did not in a five-week mindfulness training program trial for 14 to 19-year-olds.

Rest well. For both physical and emotional health, sleep is crucial. Experts advise nine to twelve hours of sleep per night for children aged six to twelve. Teens need eight to ten hours of sleep per night. To keep stress under control, sleep must come first. Limit screen time at night and avoid using electronics in bed to protect your sleep.

Step Outdoors. One of the best ways to reduce stress and enhance general well-being is to spend time in nature. According to research, those who live in locations with more green space experience less stress, anxiety, and depression.

Write a piece on it. Writing about oneself is said to help reduce mental discomfort and improve wellbeing. Writing about positive emotions, such as what you're thankful for or proud of, may reduce the symptoms of anxiety and sadness, according to several studies.

Make time for relaxation and fun. Whether it's unplanned time to play with basic building block or unbroken hours to practice music or art, children and teenagers need space to do what brings them joy. Both children and teenagers should be aware of this. Furthermore, although some youngsters like transitioning between activities, others need more leisure. Maintain a healthy balance between your free time and recreational activities.

Exercise. For people of all ages, exercise is a crucial form of stress reduction. According to the Department of Health, children ages 7 to 18 should engage in physical activity for at least 50 minutes each day.

o **How can Parents Help?**

By establishing healthy habits and assisting kids and teenagers in finding stress-relieving techniques, parents and other caregivers can play a significant role in the family's health. Parents can take the following steps:

Allow children to solve problems. It's normal to desire to help your child with their issues. However, when parents jump in to fix every small issue, their kids are deprived of the opportunity to develop effective coping mechanisms. Allowing your kids to attempt to resolve their low-stakes difficulties independently will give them more self-assurance that they can handle pressure and disappointments.

Encouraging media literacy. Most of their time these days is spent online, where adolescents risk encountering problematic material, cyberbullying, or peer pressure through social media. Parents may assist by limiting screen time and educating their kids on how to be informed digital consumers.

Fend off pessimistic thinking. "I'm not good at math. I despise my hair. I'm not going to make the team. Why even try?" Negative thinking is an easy trap for children and teenagers to slip into. Contradicting negative self-talk in children is not enough, though. Remind them of times they worked hard and got better, or challenge them to consider whether what they are saying is true. They will become more resilient to stress if they learn to frame things favorably.

3.4 Activities and Worksheets to Manage Stress

Use the following activities to deal with your stress.

How Am I Feeling

How am I Feeling?

The emotion that best describes me right now is:

I feel because _____

Some of the sensations I feel are:

It is a........
Positive   Negative
feeling
That's why I'm going to

My Reflection

<u>Things That Cause Me Stress</u>

What are the things that cause me stress?

In each oval, add something that is a stressor to you.

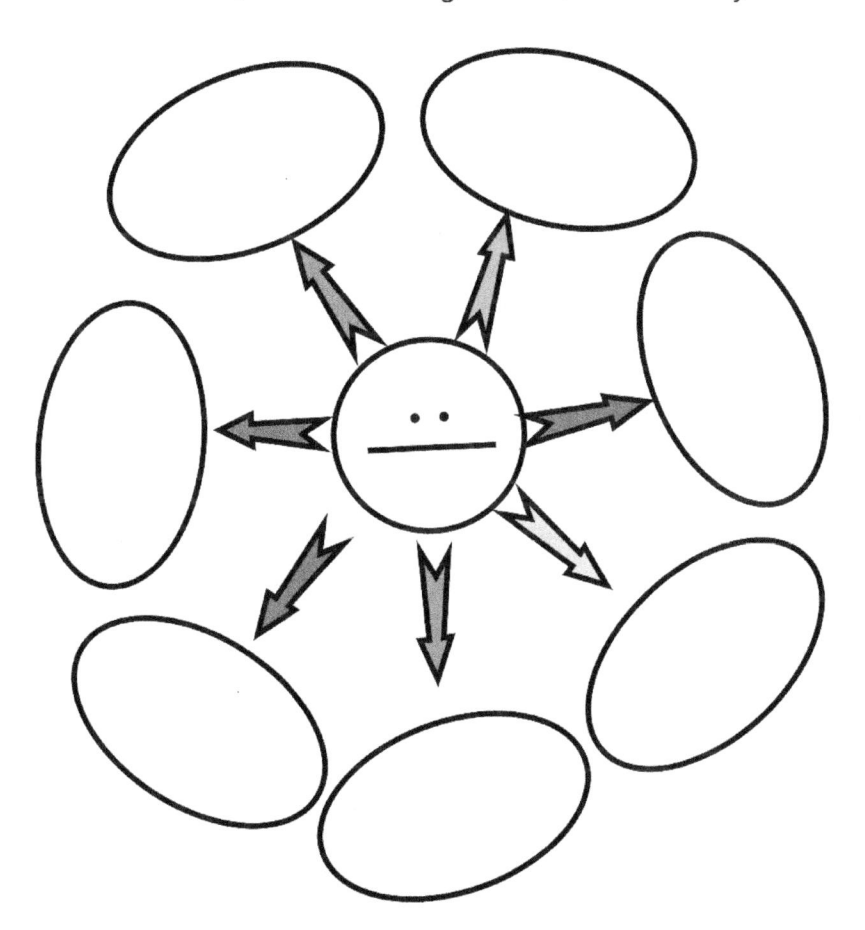

Stress Management Reflection

Stress Management Reflection

Coping Skills that work for me....

Coping Skills I have tried that don't work well for me.....

Stress Management is important because.....

Dealing with My Worries

When I felt DISAPPOINTED, these thoughts raced through my head:

Anger Thermometer

Write 2 things or situations that make you feel each of the emotions listed below.

Furious

1. _____
_____
2. _____
_____

Angry

1. _____
_____
2. _____
_____

Frustrated

1. _____
_____
2. _____
_____

Calm

1. _____
_____
2. _____
_____

When I Feel Angry

WHEN I FEEL ANGRY

I THINK....(What are some thoughts that go through your head whenever you feel angry?)

I SAY....(What are some things you say to others whenever you feel angry?)

I DO....(What are some behaviors you display whenever you feel angry?)

What are some things you can think, say or do instead?

My Stress Journal

Stress Journal

Before you can deal with stress, you must learn to recognize what causes it. Think about last week and list as many events as you can remember that caused you stress. Use the chart below to record the stressful events. Include all the information that will help you determine if there is a pattern to your stress. This journal will help you recognize what causes the most stress in your life. Be sure to rate each event as "high", "medium", or "low." Think of your reaction to the stress. For example, Did your Heart start to proud? or Did you feel your temperature rise? Write your reaction in the space provided. Now, think of some ways to relieve the stress so you can keep your cool!

Date	Time	Event (who, what, where)	Stress Level (high, medium, low)	My Reaction

CHAPTER 4

PANIC ATTACK: A FRIGHTENING EXPERIENCE

Panic attacks can be quite frightful for kids who are experiencing them and for parents who are observing them. Although they can start at any time during childhood, they usually start during puberty. These episodes can last anywhere between 10 to fifteen minutes, and they can result in a number of symptoms. You can teach your child more about panic attacks and comfort them that even while the physical symptoms may be scary, they are not harmful or life-threatening.

Teenagers who are anxious are more susceptible to panic attacks, which are terrifying since they can occur at any time. The physical symptoms of a panic attack, which is a sudden and significant rise in anxiety, include a racing heart, dizziness, numbness, and shortness of breath. The physical symptoms are an adaptive response to the perception of imminent danger. Sadly, regular stressors like a child having to take a challenging test can cause them to grow.

You can still assist your child or teen even while they are having a panic attack. Being comforting and showing empathy are essential components. Reassure them that the panic attack will pass quickly and attempt to get them to focus on something else that can create fun. The benefits of exercise, video games, TV, practicing breathing techniques, and other pleasurable hobbies are numerous.

Children might attempt to delay leaving the house or going to school in order to avoid having a panic attack. You should urge your child to continue with their everyday routines connected to school and social activities to make sure that the fear of a panic attack does not hinder their normal development.

How can you help your anxious teen stop having panic attacks?

4.1 Symptoms of a Panic Attack

Panic attack signs and symptoms include:

- Intense apprehension (a sense that something terrible is happening)
- A hammering or erratic heartbeat
- Unsteadiness or faintness
- Breathing difficulties or a suffocating sensation
- Shaking or trembling
- A feeling of unreality
- Fear of passing away, losing control, or going insane

The panic disorder will affect more than 3 million Americans at some point in their lives. Although it can start in childhood, panic disorder typically manifests during adolescence and occasionally runs in families.

Panic disorder and its consequences can have devastating effects if not identified and treated. A youngster or adolescent's relationships, academic performance, and normal growth might be hampered by panic attacks. Attacks can influence a child's mood or functioning in numerous ways, in addition to causing significant anxiety. Even when they are not experiencing panic episodes, children and adolescents with panic disorder may start to feel anxious most of the time. Some people start avoiding situations where they think a panic attack might happen or where there might not be aid accessible. A child might, for instance, be reluctant to attend school or be away from their parents. In extreme circumstances, the kid or teen might be scared to leave the house. Agoraphobia is a pattern of avoiding specific locations or circumstances, like other anxiety disorders. Some kids and teenagers with panic disorder may experience extreme depression and even consider suicide. Some adolescent sufferers of panic disorder will use alcohol or drugs to reduce anxiety.

4.2 Causes of Panic in Teens

Repeated, sporadic panic attacks that can leave sufferers with feelings of great anxiety, separation from reality, and even impending death characterize the panic disorder. The family of anxiety disorders includes panic disorder. People with panic disorder often have symptoms between adolescence and early adulthood. Even though there isn't a single known cause of panic disorder in teenagers, doctors and researchers offer a few theories.

Genetics: Studies involving identical twins have shown a substantial likelihood of a hereditary component to panic disorder.

Chemical imbalances in the brain are connected to postulated (and well-supported) probable causes of panic disorder, including *brain chemistry*. The neurotransmitters dopamine, serotonin, and norepinephrine tend to be less abundant in those who experience panic episodes and panic disorder, according to research. Furthermore, there is a significant correlation between panic disorder and having an "overactive" amygdala, the area of the brain in charge of controlling the fight-or-flight response.

Environment: According to some research, stress levels and one's upbringing are two environmental factors that may contribute to panic attacks in teenagers and young adults.

Various risk factors can raise one's chances of getting panic disorder, regardless of whether a youngster is predisposed to it due to genetics, stress, neurochemistry, or environment. These risk factors include:

- Receiving a mental health diagnosis, such as depression, anxiety, or bipolar disorder

- A teen is more likely to develop a panic disorder or experience panic episodes if they have certain health issues, such as asthma or other respiratory issues.
- High-stress levels
- Enduring a painful experience
- Significant loss or change in life

4.3 Helping Teens with Panic Disorder

Both panic disorder and panic attacks can be treated.

Several treatment techniques and approaches may be suggested depending on how severely panic attacks are interfering with a teen's life and everyday functioning. Typical techniques for managing panic attacks include:

For adolescents and teenagers who experience panic attacks or panic disorder, the most frequently given drugs are benzodiazepines and selective serotonin inhibitors (SSRIs). _SSRIs_ have been successfully used in research to treat kids with panic disorder, although it can take three to six weeks before they start working. Panic symptoms are immediately and briefly relieved by benzodiazepines. They are typically prescribed "as needed," which allows the patient to decide when and how much to take medicine. Sadly, benzodiazepines have the potential to develop a dependency. Usually, a suggestion for psychotherapy is made along with a medication prescription.

A frequent strategy used in psychotherapy, particularly for panic episodes and anxiety attacks, is _cognitive-behavioral therapy_ (CBT). Cognitive restructuring and exposition and response planning are both used in cognitive behavioral therapy. A teen who is experiencing panic attacks can learn to recognize and start managing their thoughts with the use of this therapeutic technique. Additionally, CBT offers helpful coping mechanisms and methods for overcoming unreasonable anxieties.

Group therapy - group forms of treatment for anxious and panicky teenagers have undergone substantial research. Several factors contribute to group therapy's effectiveness, including the chance for peer modeling, social support, and the reinforcement of positive behaviors and coping mechanisms.

Biofeedback, also known as applied psychophysiological feedback, helps clients learn to control body functions like heart rate by using electronic monitoring. Electrical sensors attached to the person getting the biofeedback provide information (feedback) about their body (bio). The approach enables the person experiencing panic to see how their bodies react to stress and anxiety. They can then manage actions and brain activity resulting from that awareness. Biofeedback has been thoroughly studied in treating anxiety disorders and is an effective therapy option, particularly for people who do not wish to utilize medication.

Whether or not your adolescent decides to seek professional help for their panic attacks, it's crucial to teach them stress management techniques that they can employ on their own, independently of any other treatments. Deep breathing, muscle relaxation, and recognizing and rebuking unhelpful thoughts are a few examples of coping mechanisms.

4.4 Activities and Worksheets to Control Panic Attacks

Here are some activities worksheets to control panic attacks.

My Panic Symptoms

My Panic Symptoms

List your personal experiences with anxiety and panic

Physical symptoms

Panic Thoughts

Avoidance Behaviors

Panic Assessment

What were you **thinking** about before your most recent panic attack?

How were you **feeling** before your most recent panic attack?

What were you **doing** before your most recent panic attack?

Circle the symptoms you experience during panic attacks.		
Pounding or racing heart	Difficulty breathing	Sweating
Sense of terror, impending doom, or death	Feeling dizzy, light-headed, or faint	Feeling of being detached from reality or oneself
Fear of "going crazy"	Nausea	Chest pain or discomfort
Choking sensation	Chills or feeling of heat	Numbness or tingling
Trembling or shaking	Other	

Are you worried about having another panic attack?

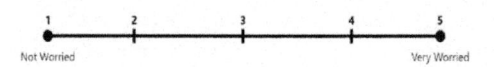

1 — 2 — 3 — 4 — 5
Not Worried   Very Worried

How would you rate the discomfort caused by your panic attacks?

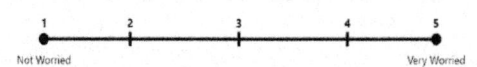

1 — 2 — 3 — 4 — 5
Not Worried   Very Worried

Have you changed your behavior because of your past panic attacks?
Example: Avoiding situations that you think might cause a panic attack, or places where a panic attack would be embarrassing a dangerous.

☐ Yes
☐ No

My Subconscious Expectations

My Subconscious Expectations

For this exercise, write the first things that come to mind for each questions. Try not to overthink it!

What are your favorite parts of your current life? Which of those do you want to keep as a part of your adult life?

_____
_____
_____
_____
_____
_____
_____
_____
_____
_____

Imagine yourself as an adult who is not married. What does your life look like?

_____
_____
_____
_____
_____
_____
_____
_____
_____
_____

Imagine raising your own children. What do you want their life to be like?

_____
_____
_____
_____
_____
_____
_____
_____
_____
_____

Imagine being 90 years old, When you look back, what would you like to say you did as an adult?

_____
_____
_____
_____
_____
_____
_____
_____
_____
_____

Problem Solving

Problem Solving

When an event happens, what you think will affect what you feel and what you do.

Situation

Describe the situation:
_____
_____
_____

Thoughts

What were your thoughts?
_____
_____
_____

Feelings

How did you feel?
_____
_____
_____

Behavior

What were your behaviors(how did you react?):
_____
_____
_____

Outcome

What was the outcome?
_____
_____
_____

I am Someone Who

I Am Someone Who....

Complete the sentences below to share more about yourself!

I am someone who loves _____

I am someone who hates _____

I am someone who can't _____

I am someone who can _____

I am someone who will never _____

I am someone who has _____

I am someone who can't wait to _____

I am someone who would rather _____ than _____

I am someone who has never _____

I am someone who wishes _____

I am someone who tried to _____

I am someone whom nobody seems to _____

I am someone whom everybody seems to _____

I am someone who just can't get enough _____

I am someone who doesn't know how to _____

I am someone who usually forgets to _____

I am someone who never forgets to _____

I am someone who is thankful for _____

I am someone who will probably end up _____

I am _____

CHAPTER 5

LIVING HEALTHILY: EXPRESS THE EMOTIONS YOU FEEL

The last period is on a Friday afternoon. In precisely 4 hours, the weekend getaway you and your friend have planned will begin. You've spent the entire week catching up on work and schoolwork so you can enjoy your vacation. Now the instructor says that there will be an exam on Monday. You're undoubtedly irritated or perhaps even furious. You may experience disappointment. You can also experience anxiety or tension due to how much effort you will have to put in to perform well.

But what is your response? How do you act and speak?

You might want to scream at the teacher by standing up. "That is unfair! Some of us are busy this weekend." However, you are aware that you must maintain your composure until the end of class, at which point you can talk to your friend about how you are feeling.

What if, though, you're not the cool, or kind?

Not to worry. Everyone can learn how to react appropriately when their emotions are running high. For some folks, it simply requires a little more practice.

5.1 Learning to React Well

Making decisions about when and how to express our emotions is known as managing our emotional reactions. It's important to express your emotions, but how (and when) you do so matters. People who are adept at controlling their emotions are aware of this. As a result, they can respond to circumstances in useful ways:

- They know they have control over how they respond and don't have to let their feelings lead them to say or do something they would later regret.
- They know when it is beneficial to express themselves and when it is preferable to hold off on doing so.
- They are aware that their actions impact what follows, including how others perceive them and how they feel about themselves.

You've probably had situations where someone responded overly emotionally, causing you to cringe or feel bad for them. Additionally, you may have encountered circumstances in which your emotions were so strong that it required all of your willpower to refrain from following them.

Perhaps you can recall an instance in which you reacted inappropriately. Perhaps you were overcome by fear, rage, or frustration. It occurs. When it does, be kind to yourself and consider how you may have done things differently. Consider your options for the foreseeable future.

The abilities we use to control our emotions and respond appropriately are a subset of a larger category of emotional abilities known as emotional intelligence (EQ). It takes time and repetition to master all the abilities that make up emotional intelligence.

Some foundational EQ skills are already strong in those who react well. But everyone can cultivate these abilities:

Emotional intelligence. Recognizing and naming the feelings we are experiencing at any particular time is the key to mastering this ability. It is the most fundamental EQ ability. Sometimes all it takes to feel more in control of our emotions is to name the emotion we are experiencing.

Recognizing and accepting feelings. Knowing the causes of our feelings allows us to manage them better. Saying to ourselves, "I feel left out and a little nervous because I didn't get invited to the prom yet, while two of my friends already did," is one example of what we could say to ourselves.

It is beneficial to see our feelings as reasonable according to the circumstances. It's understandable to feel left out in this circumstance; we could think to ourselves. It is like showing ourselves a little compassion and tolerance for how we are feeling. This enables us to accept our feelings. We understand that they make sense and that it is acceptable for us to feel however we choose.

Accepting emotions is seeing, recognizing, and comprehending them without placing blame on others or critiquing oneself. Telling ourselves how we feel is someone else's fault is not helpful. The thoughts "I shouldn't feel this way" or "It's terrible that I feel this way" are not healthy responses to our feelings. The objective is to acknowledge your emotions without allowing them to control you.

You'll be better able to control what you do when experiencing powerful emotions if these fundamental skills become second nature. Using the fundamental techniques, you can move through challenging emotions more quickly.

5.2 What Would You Do?

Imagine the following scenario: Your pals have sent you prom invitations (or college acceptances, team places, etc.). However, you haven't. How might you respond once you've recognized, comprehended, and accepted how you feel?

- When you're among your friends, try to appear upset, so they'll ask you what's wrong.
- Make sarcastic remarks about others who have made plans and declare your disinterest in attending the pointless dance.

- Be open with a friend, "I regret not having been asked yet. I can, however, still go with pals."

Keep in mind that everything is not lost. Choose to be patient and refrain from letting it spoil your day. Think about each option and what might happen in each case. Which response would produce the best result?

We can always choose how to respond to circumstances. Making good decisions is simpler once we are aware of that. It takes practice to become a good reactor. But there is always room for improvement when managing our emotions and letting them out in constructive ways. And that's a positive thing to think about!

5.3 Handle The Roller Coaster of Emotions

In my practice, there has been a recent rise in parents contacting their children to assist with emotional regulation. Parents frequently tell me, "My teen jumps from 0 to 60, seemingly out of the blue. I have no apparent way to help. There is no effect of discipline."

I believe it is important to remember that most of us would not want to go back to our adolescent years. The numerous changes that occur all at once—physical, emotional, and life—are challenging to handle. The teenage years are a time of fast brain development, which triggers the limbic system's fight, flight or freeze response. When the brain operates in this mode, it has limited access to executive abilities like reason, logic, and good judgment.

In addition, it is crucial to consider the numerous challenges that life places in a teen's path because they may cause trauma, anxiety, sadness, or general distress. Teenagers have a lot on their plates, having to deal with social circumstances, bullies, and other stressors, school, a variety of other duties, home life, and starting (or continuing) the journey of self-discovery.

The Technique of an Empty Chair

Gestalt philosophy is the source of the empty chair technique, which is cathartic in letting go of emotions and identifying internal conflict. Teens with emotional dysregulation often metaphorically place the person or situation they are struggling with into an empty chair. The teenager assumes the other person's position by sitting in the chair and speaking as they might. The teen then returns to their chair and speaks their thoughts aloud to the individual or people they would like to share their sentiments with.

I advise kids not to be concerned with what they are saying when using this method. They are free to yell if necessary. Without fear of reprisal, they are free to express their unfiltered sentiments. This exercise aims to make the kid more aware of the internal conflict they are going through about the other person or circumstance.

Taking Feelings into Acceptance

Teenagers must learn how to accept their emotions. Teenagers I work with frequently ask me for advice on dealing with their volatile emotions. I occasionally ponder what would happen if you acknowledged your feelings? Accepting sentiments is not a strategy that is frequently considered.

I tell the kids that feelings aren't always biased. Teenagers who give in to their emotions, risk losing perspective on what is true because emotions can obscure the big picture. I frequently counsel teenagers to be aware of their self-talk. How do they describe their feelings to themselves? Self-talk is extremely potent, and most use it more negatively than positively.

The same applies to teenagers. However, I advise young people to permit themselves to feel things, to be present in the moment, and to "be" with all of their feelings, even the unpleasant ones. Teens must develop self-soothing skills and the ability to process their emotions mindfully and intentionally to do this. Teenagers are urged to permit themselves to feel, to be present in the moment, and to "be" with all of their emotions, even the unpleasant ones. Teens must develop self-soothing skills and the ability to process their emotions mindfully and intentionally to do this.

Teenagers frequently deal with situations outside of their control, which can lead to anxiety rooted in dread. Uncontrollable things can cause fear. Teenagers may find it helpful to learn how to discern and then let go of what cannot be managed because it is crucial to know what can be controlled and what cannot. This is undoubtedly much easier said than done!

I also support teens finding healthy ways to communicate their good and negative emotions. Teens must learn to release their emotions in healthy ways that won't damage them or others. Feelings must be released in some way.

- Teenagers can express their emotions in a variety of suitable ways, including:
- Teenagers can express their emotions via writing.
- Teenagers can use art to communicate their emotions.
- Many teenagers discover and express their emotions through music.
- Teenagers can benefit from engaging in physical activity to help them express their emotions.
- Teenagers should understand that it's okay to cry since crying may sometimes be quite helpful.

Gaining perspective and letting go of sentiments can be facilitated by talking about and processing emotions with a trustworthy person. Teenagers occasionally need to "simply be" and release some of their pressure. This ought to be permitted and promoted.

Get It Out (Healthy)

Trying to suppress or ignore your emotions can only make matters worse. You shouldn't dismiss the message your emotions are trying to convey. Even if suppressing those sensations temporarily makes you feel better, you will still be experiencing those emotions. Stomach aches or worse can result from holding in your emotions.

It is healthy for you, so get it out of your system while you can! In particular, weeping causes your body to release endorphins and the "feel-good" hormone oxytocin. They lessen your mental and bodily suffering. A nice weep will make you feel better. Here are some alternative methods of crying that you can try:

Exercise. You can skateboard, ride a bike, box, run, lift weights, surf, or engage in any other activity that will help you let go of those endorphins and stored energy.

Play your favorite music as you go. Your mood can be improved by dancing, head banging, and having fun, such as at karaoke.

Engage in a hobby you enjoy. Making fun videos for social media, engaging in a sport, fidgeting with a hobby, or playing a fun activity help you to let out things in mind.

Unwind. A soothing activity might provide you time to relax and get past your sentiments, whether taking a bath, baking, or even cleaning.

Spread Out

Nobody can successfully navigate life on their own. Now and then, we could all use some help. It is not a show of weakness to spread out to a family member. It's a sign of strength, emotional health, and self-assurance. It's the aspect of "adulting" that even many people still struggle with.

Your stress can be reduced by talking to someone. Additionally, it can help you feel better when someone acknowledges how you're feeling and validates it. Having a conversation with a friend, a member of your family, or a therapist might also help you gain perspective. That person will frequently even assist you in finding answers to your problems. The benefits of therapy make it the best choice.

As long as you don't indicate any imminent risk to yourself or others, therapists are required by law to keep all information confidential and not disclose it to your parents or anyone else.

5.4 Activities and Worksheets to Control Emotions

Try the following activities to control your emotions effectively.

Feelings and Emotions

Feelings and Emotions

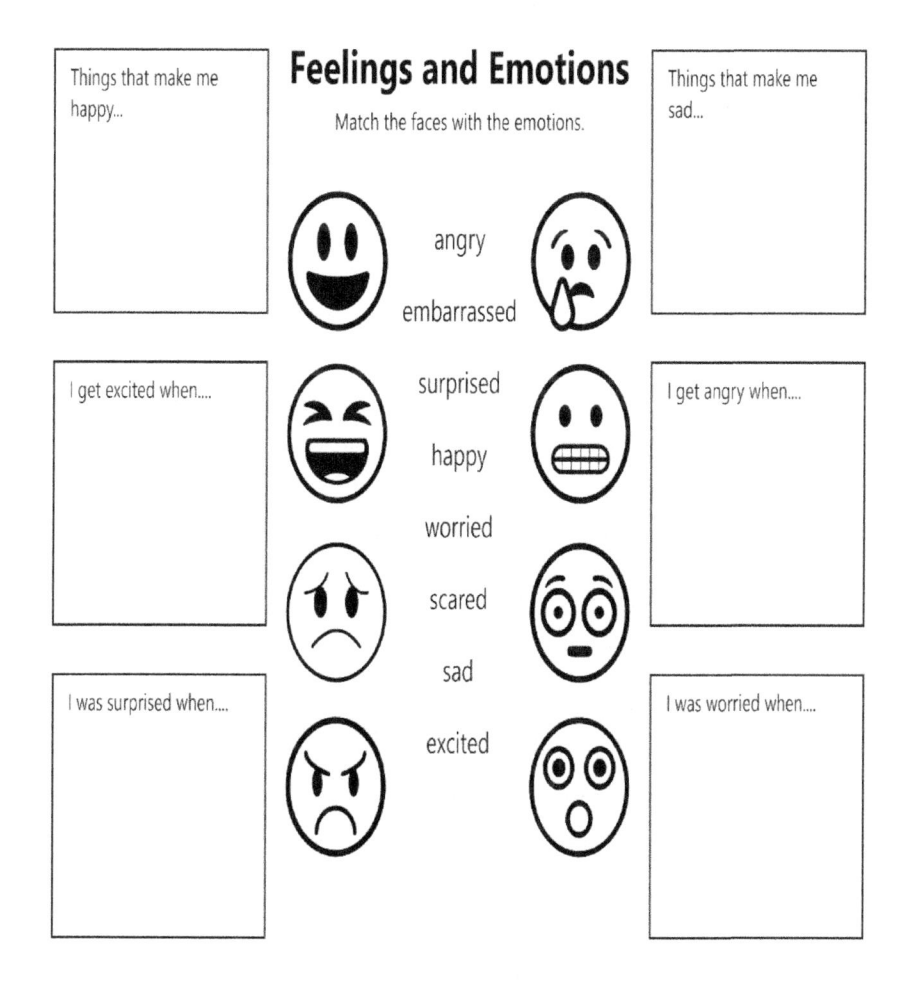

Match the faces with the emotions.

Things that make me happy...

Things that make me sad...

angry

embarrassed

surprised

happy

worried

scared

sad

excited

I get excited when....

I get angry when....

I was surprised when....

I was worried when....

Emotions Worksheet

Emotions

Emotions are our feelings we have over things that happen

1. What makes you mad?
_____
_____
_____

[paste]

2. Name a time you felt afraid -
_____
_____
_____

[paste]

3. What makes you happy?
_____
_____
_____

[paste]

4. Name a time you felt sad -
_____
_____
_____

[paste]

Cut out the picture below and glue them in the appropriate box above

Inside Out: Getting to Know My Emotions

My emotion	Feels like	Sounds Like	A memory when I felt....
Sadness			
Disgust			
Joy			
Anger			
Fear			

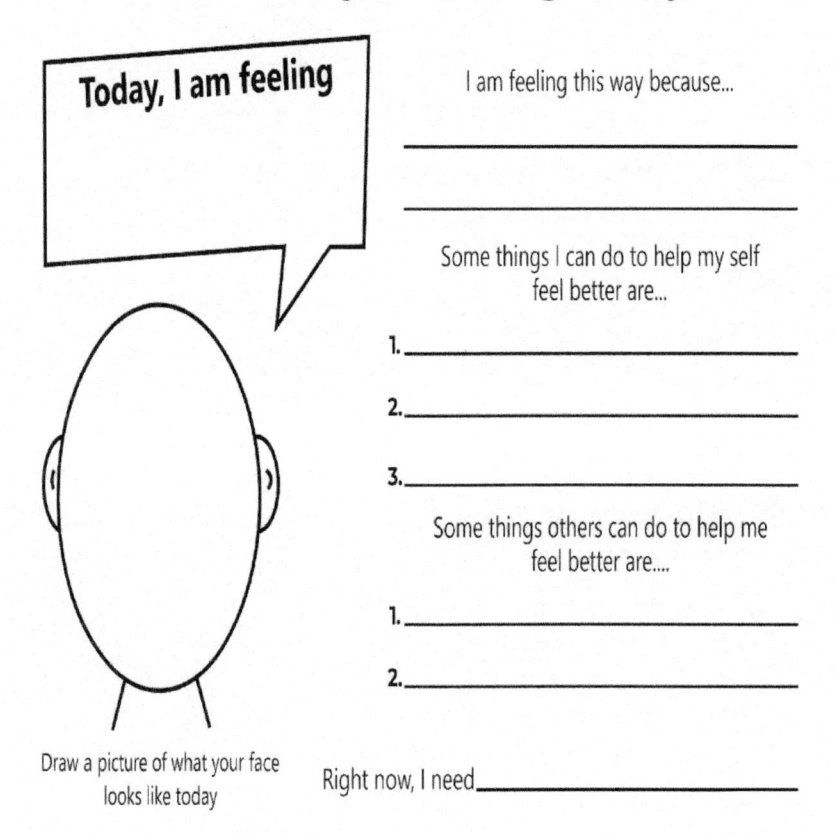

How Are You Feeling Today?

How are you feeling today?

Today, I am feeling

Draw a picture of what your face looks like today

I am feeling this way because...

_____

_____

Some things I can do to help my self feel better are...

1._____

2._____

3._____

Some things others can do to help me feel better are....

1._____

2._____

Right now, I need_____

When I Feel Sad

WHEN I FEEL SAD

I THINK....
(What are some thoughts that go through your head whenever you feel sad?)

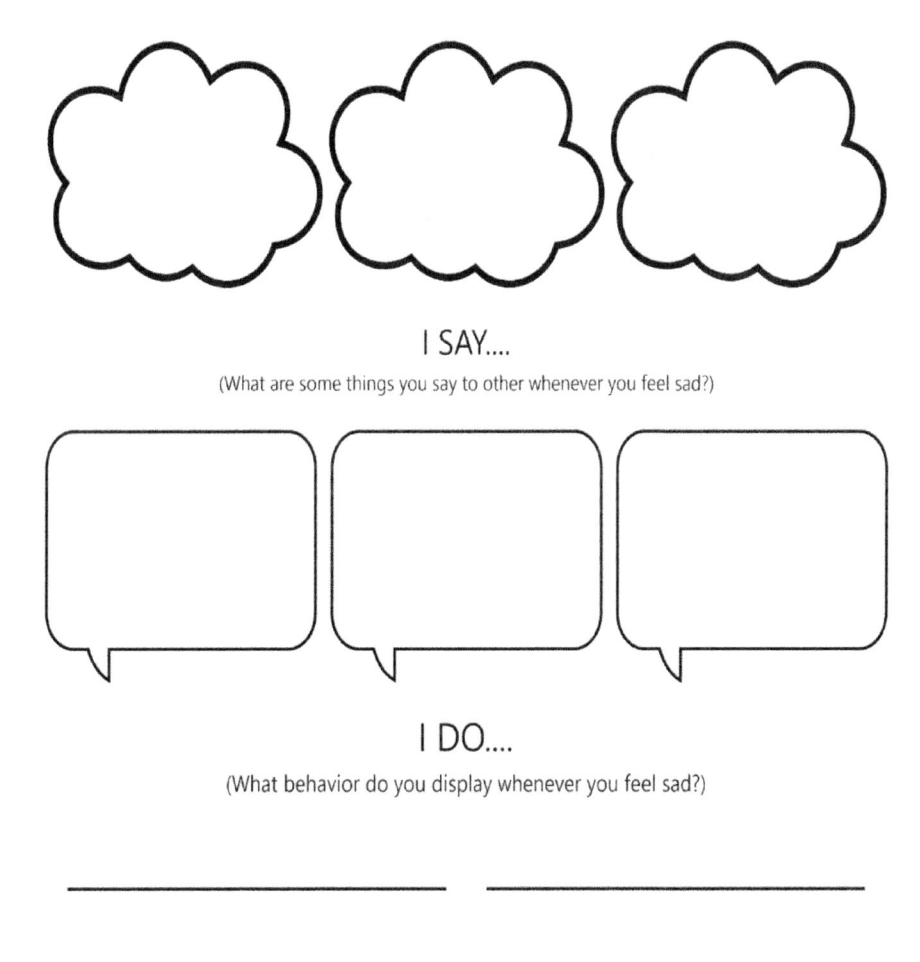

I SAY....
(What are some things you say to other whenever you feel sad?)

I DO....
(What behavior do you display whenever you feel sad?)

_____   _____

_____   _____

When I Felt...

When I Felt _____

Draw a picture of a time you experienced this feeling!

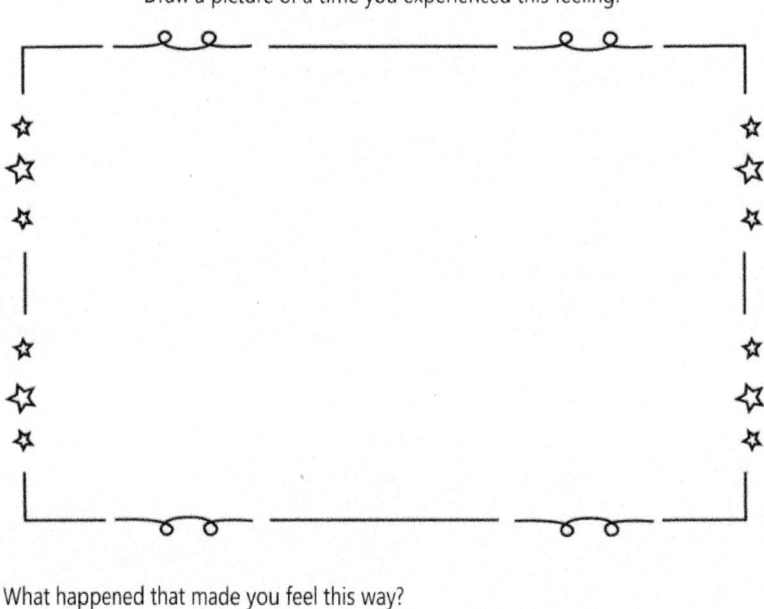

What happened that made you feel this way?

_____

_____

Was it a good feeling? **YES** or **NO**

What did other people do when they saw you feeling this way?

_____

_____

What did you do to cope with this feeling?

_____

_____

All Feelings Are Okay

All Feelings are Okay!

In the circles below draw pictures of different feelings.
Talk about how you can deal with each feelings!

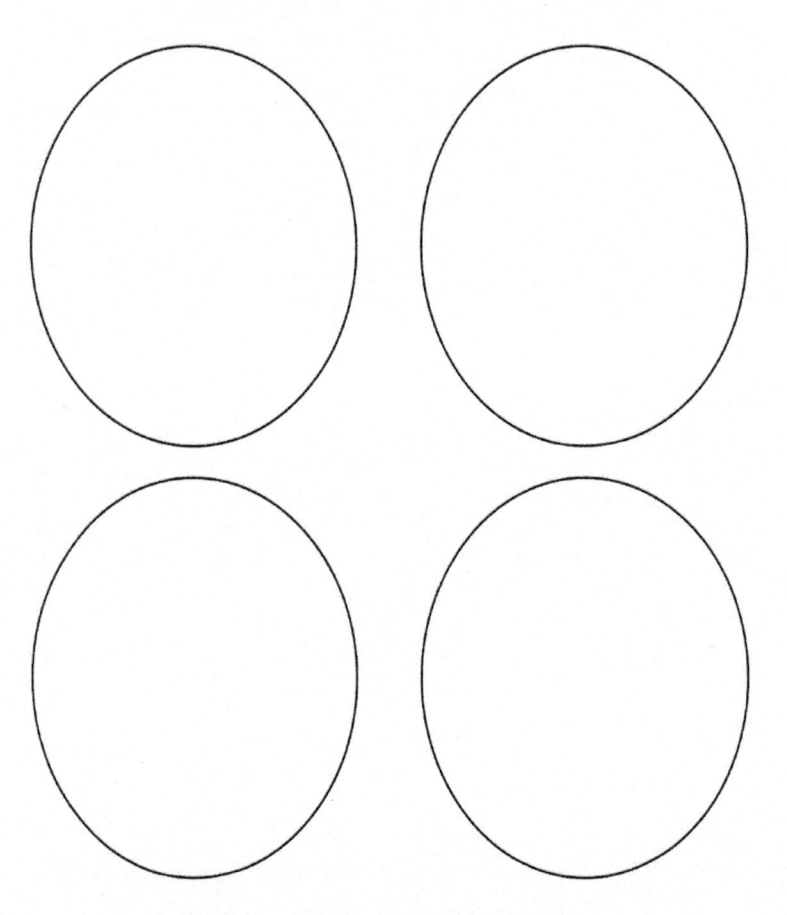

It's what we do with our feelings that counts!

Never use your feelings as an excuse to hurt others or yourself! Use coping skills like talking to a friend or an adult about BIG feelings that trouble you!

Coping with Feelings

Coping with Feelings

Use this worksheet to come up with coping skills for the different feelings below!

When I'm feeling _____ I can _____

Something that makes me feel angry is _____

When I'm feeling _____ I can _____

Something that makes me feel sad is _____

When I'm feeling _____ I can _____

Something that makes me feel scared is _____

When I'm feeling _____ I can _____

Something that makes me feel hurt is _____

When I'm feeling _____ I can _____

Something that makes me feel worried is _____

5.5 Meditation and Mindfulness Activities

Regardless of your age, mastering the inner turmoil that life invariably delivers is no simple task. Teenagers have additional difficulties, however, due to hormonal changes, a still-developing brain, the intensity of peer interactions, academic pressures, and their parents' high expectations. And if they're lucky, that is! Many teenagers also battle with problems with their bodies, poor relationships with their families, and an overreliance on technology rather than human interaction. Their mental health may therefore deteriorate. Teens who lack the coping mechanisms to deal with life's ups and downs may also develop teen depression, anxiety disorders, eating disorders, and substance use disorders.

Teenagers need accessible, long-lasting tools that help them learn to express their emotions without giving in to despair, rage, fear, or bewilderment. The good news is that every youngster can use those tools. The secret is to develop straightforward, regular routines that support happiness and balance rather than a magic formula or magic pill.

A person's ability to accomplish goals is likely hindered by fluctuating emotional states and insufficient self-control. For instance, a child who struggles with anger management would elicit unfavorable responses from others and feel even more isolated or rejected. In contrast, a systematic approach to managing anger has the opposite effect and encourages social participation, stability, and cooperation.

o **Peaceful Strolls**

Set aside time to walk in your area a few times per week and look for new things. During the stroll, set aside one minute to stay entirely silent and pay attention to the colors and sounds you can hear, such as birds, lawnmowers, dogs, and so on.

Mindfulness
1. Start by imagining anything that makes you feel anxious, but not excessively so.
2. Take a moment to relax your body's muscles by sitting comfortably and keeping your eyes closed or slightly fixed on the ground.
3. Make the anxious circumstance conscious in your mind. To remain rooted in the present moment, focus some of your attention on your breathing.
4. As you keep the anxious circumstance in your awareness, pay attention to everything that transpires in your body and thoughts. Here, the aim is to pique your curiosity.

Which feeling does your body experience? What ideas cross your mind? What transpires with time? Does the situation remain clear in your mind, or does it get hazy?

Keep in mind that nothing needs to be altered or fixed. If you find that your automatic thoughts are taking over, gently return your focus to the breath and the present moment.

- **Mindfulness to Improve Self-Awareness and Self-Esteem**
    1. Get comfy and begin by concentrating on your breath. After that, broaden your awareness to include every bodily sensation, the sound you hear, idea, and emotion you are experiencing.
    2. Given that the mind can never be satisfied with itself, how does this affect some of your most ingrained beliefs and sense of self? Spend some time reflecting on these questions.
    3. You can discover that you primarily identify who you are based on important memories and automatic thought processes, which is an inaccurate perspective.
    4. Finish the exercise by paying close attention to your breathing for a few minutes.

5. To finish your practice, pay attention to the breath for a few minutes.

Anxiety can sometimes go away fast, and other times it can linger. The objective is to become conscious of your automatic thought processes and identify distortions. Additionally, mindfulness can assist you in realizing that the feelings connected to your anxiety are not all that difficult to cope with and that they seem to vanish when you invite the feared circumstance to be present.

- **Mindfulness to Reduce Anger and Irritability**
    1. Start by imagining a circumstance that would make you angry. Pick one that makes you feel annoyed or frustrated but not enraged or furious.
    2. Concentrate on your breath, then broaden your awareness to take in all of your environment's auditory and physical sensations.
    3. At this point, bring the situation that makes you angry to your attention. Observe any reactions in your body or mind for around three minutes while focusing on the scenario.
    4. Permit your feelings and thoughts to come and go like clouds in the sky.
    5. Finish the practice by refocusing on your breathing for a minute or two.

- **A Report About My Weather**

Keep calm and take note of your surroundings and internal environment. It aids in the discovery of your thoughts, feelings, and actions. As you breathe in and out, pay attention to your breathing. Feel your belly and chest expand. Stay still, quiet and unhurried. Spend some time concentrating your attention. Start noticing the little things. Just be aware of certain motions. Consider your current emotions as a weather report right now. Sunshine, thunder, rain, calm, tornado...? Simply consider and pay attention to your emotions. You are unable to alter your feelings, just like the weather. However, you can change how you react to it. Your emotions and feelings are not who you are. They change, just like the weather does. Simply embrace them as they come.

- **A Habit of Gratitude**

Before a meal, everyone participates in spending a moment each day to thank someone or something. It significantly enhances sympathy for others and fosters good consciousness. The capacity to control emotions and maintain emotional equilibrium is associated with compassion.

- **Mindfulness to Reduce Anxiety**
    1. Take a comfy seat. Take a moment to relax your body while you close your eyes.
    2. Start concentrating on your breathing and the bodily sensations it causes.
    3. As soon as you feel firmly rooted in the present, pay attention to any involuntary thoughts and feelings plaguing you.
    4. Recognize your thoughts and feelings without assigning them a right or wrong verdict or attempting to correct or alter anything. Permit yourself to be mindful of it.

After doing this exercise, you can find that your thinking is clearer since you have put some distance between yourself and your thoughts. You might be able to recognize that there are steps you can take to improve your mood. You can also find that there is nothing you need to do.

- **Mindfulness to Observe Your Thought Patterns**
    1. For roughly two minutes, anchor your attention on your breathing to bring your attention to the present moment. If you have any thoughts, don't try to stop them; just let them run freely in the background as you slowly return your attention to your breathing.

2. Increase awareness of your body's physical feelings and the sounds surrounding you as they emerge and fade.
3. Keep track of your thoughts. Think about lying on the grass and gazing at the clouds passing by. Watch your thoughts as they drift by picturing them as individual clouds.

Observing your ideas as they come and go won't disrupt your mind, just as the clouds aren't upsetting the sky.

- **Mindfulness to Reduce Impulsive Behavior**
    1. Begin by imagining anything that triggers some yearning but isn't overpowering.
    2. Pay attention to your breath. Then broaden your consciousness to incorporate all of your body's physical sensations.
    3. At this point, become aware of the circumstance causing your urge. For about three minutes, make an effort to remain focused on the situation.
    4. Pay attention to the thoughts that are going through your head. Is there any thinking about how satisfying it would be to give in to the compulsion? Are you feeling anything in your body? Try to observe that objectively.
    5. To complete the practice, give your breath your undivided attention for a minute or two.

Below are some exercises to let go of your thoughts, practicing mindfulness and breathing to relax for having a healthy lifestyle.

Let it Go

Write down thoughts in balloons that you want to let go.

LET IT GO

Forgiveness Fingers

Ca you follow these five rules by using your fingers?

My Forgiveness Fingers

ACCEPT

APOLOGIZE

LISTEN

BREATHE

LOVE

Gratitude Journal

EVENING GRATITUDE JOURNAL

Evening Gratitude
(list 5 things you're grateful for)

1.
2.
3.
4.
5.

What I Learned
(list 3 things you learned today)

1.
2.
3.

People who made my day great!
(list 5 people you're grateful for)

1.
2.
3.
4.
5.

Best moment of the day
(describe the best part of your day and why)

_____
_____
_____
_____
_____
_____
_____

Self-awareness happiness assessment

What type of person are you today?

_____
_____
_____
_____
_____

Describe the person that you want to become only using three verbs.

I am happiest when I ....

I am most unhappy when....

3 Things that instantly put me in a great mood.

1 Person who makes me feel motivated and inspired.

1

2 Things that make me laugh

2

3

My Learning Sheet

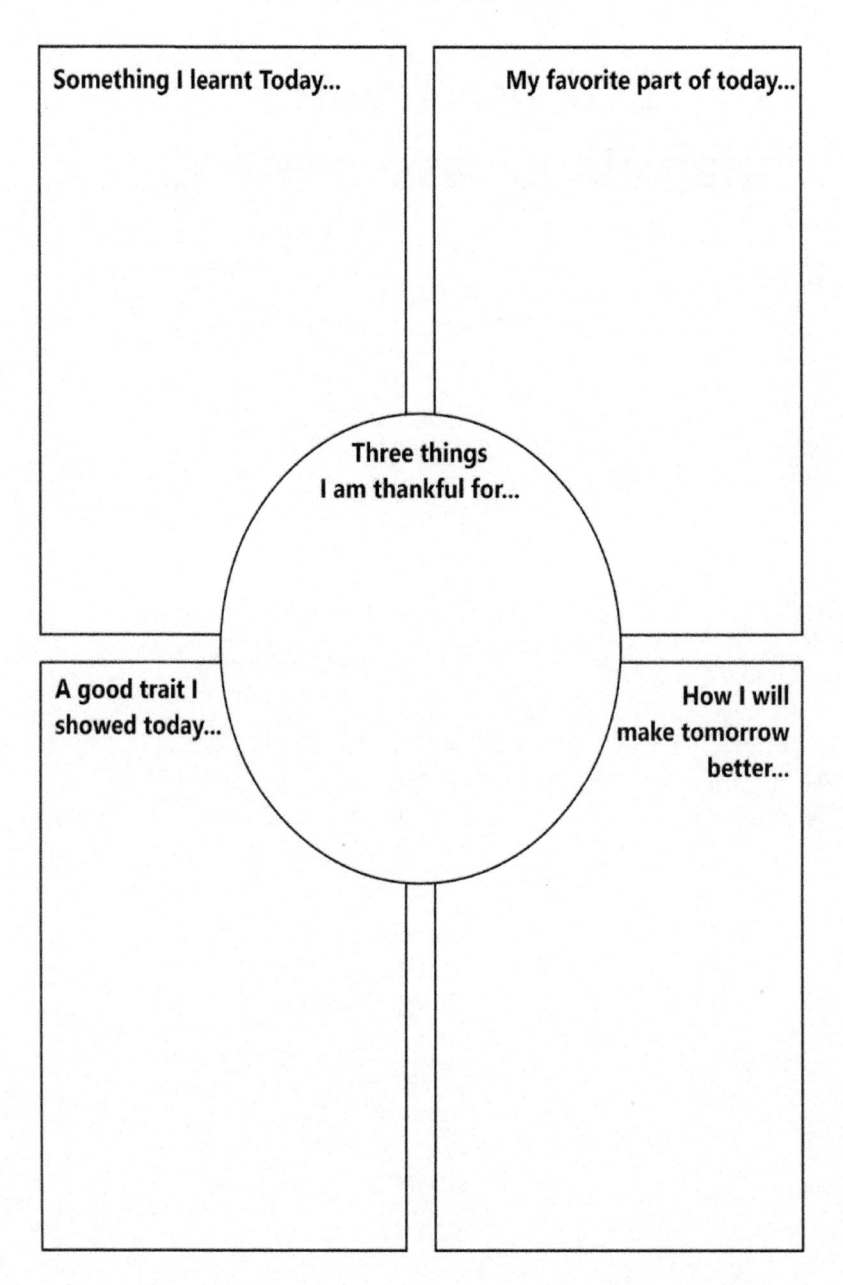

Something I learnt Today...	My favorite part of today...

Three things I am thankful for...

A good trait I showed today...	How I will make tomorrow better...

About My Day

Today's Date:_____

My Mood

Today's Weather

Something I learned today:

_____
_____
_____
_____

3 things that made me happy today
1. _____
2. _____
3. _____

3 things that I am grateful for today
1. _____
2. _____
3. _____

Growth Mindset

Growth Mindset

Strengths

What do you want your buds to turn into? How will you do this?

_____
_____
_____
_____

Rainbow Breathing

RAINBOW BREATHING
exercise

Place your finger at the bottom of the rainbow, on left.

Take a deep breath in as you move your finger half way up the first rainbow color toward the arrow.

When you reach the arrow, begin to exhale as you keep moving your finger to the end of the rainbow, on right.

Repeat with every color to help you feel calm and grounded.

Lazy 8 Breathing

Lazy 8 Breathing

Start with an 8 on its side. Starting in the middle, go up to the left and trace the left part of the 8 with your finger while you breathe in, When you get to the middle of the 8 again, breathe out while you trace the right part of the 8 with your finger.

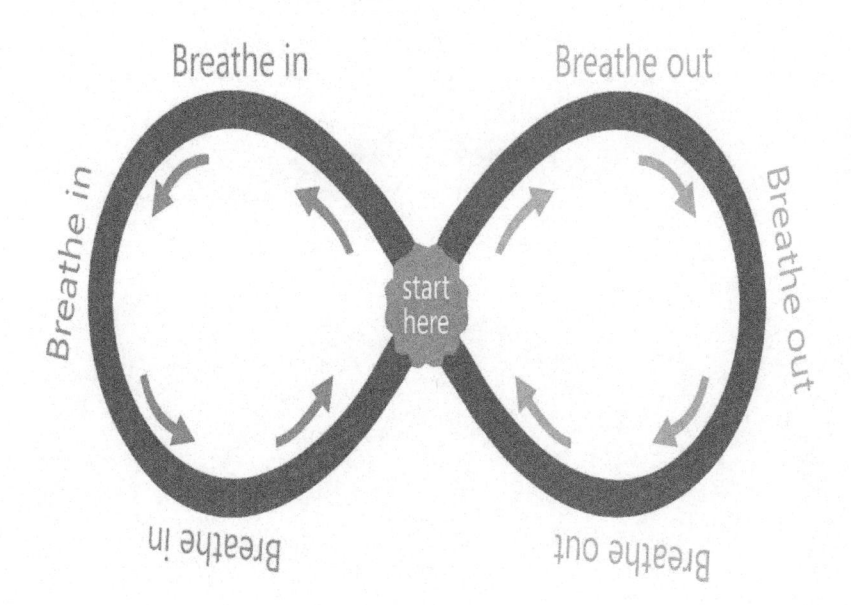

Beach Day Breath

Follow the lines of the waves breathing in and breathing out

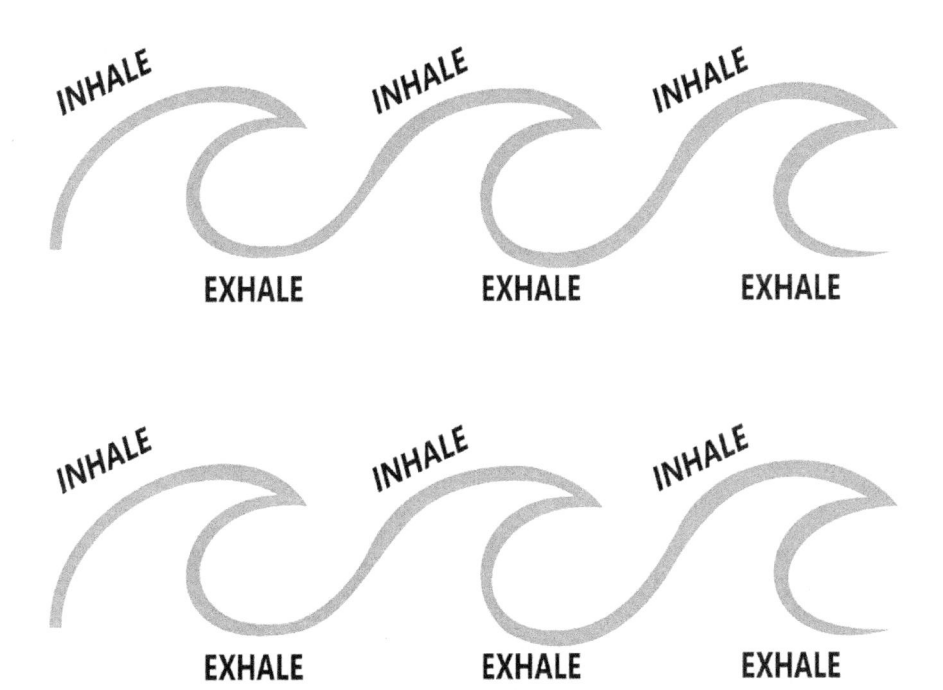

INHALE　　　　INHALE　　　　INHALE

EXHALE　　　　EXHALE　　　　EXHALE

INHALE　　　　INHALE　　　　INHALE

EXHALE　　　　EXHALE　　　　EXHALE

Dragon Breathing

Dragon Breathing

1. Hold your hand in front of your face and take a breath in through your nose.

2. As you breathe out through your mouth, whisper the world "hah."

3. Notice the way the heat of your breath feels on your hand.

4. Repeat until clam and grouded

Yoga Poses

Camel Pose	 Plow Pose	 Boat Pose
 Tree Pose	 Triangle Pose	 Belly Breathing
 Cobra Pose	 Warrior Pose	 Down Dog Pose

HOW CAN PARENTS HELP?

Everyone deals with anxiety. It is a healthy and significant emotion that warns of impending danger or a rapid, dangerous shift through feelings of apprehension, fear, and alarm. However, worry can occasionally escalate into an unhealthy reaction.

Anxiety frequently hums like background noise while a normal teenager deals with various transitions and concerns. Some teenagers have high-pitched, persistent anxiety that makes it difficult for them to go to class and perform at their best academically. It becomes challenging to engage in extracurricular activities, make and keep friends, and have a loving, flexible connection within the family. Anxiety can occasionally only manifest as vague, drifting emotions of unease. Other times, it turns into phobias and panic attacks.

o **Finding the Symptoms**

Teenagers have different anxiety issues from one another. Typical symptoms include excessive anxieties and fears, unrest inside, and a propensity to be overly cautious and watchful. Teenagers can speak of feeling restless, anxious, or extremely stressed even when there is no real threat.

Worried teenagers can appear needy, aloof, or awkward in social situations. They can behave uncooperative as either being extremely passionate or overly repressed. They can be concerned with thoughts of slipping out of control or irrational worry about their social skills.

Teenagers with severe anxiety frequently experience a variety of physical symptoms. They could express complaints about exhaustion, pubertal changes, stomachaches, headaches, pain in the limbs and back, muscle tension and cramps. They might easily blush, splotch, sweat excessively, quiver, and startle.

Adolescent anxiety frequently revolves around issues with social acceptance, changes in how the adolescent's body feels and looks, and fights over independence. Adolescents may appear incredibly bashful when they are overwhelmed with anxiety. They can refrain from doing their typical activities or reject trying something new. When they are separated from their buddies, they could object. They might also experiment with drugs, engage in dangerous activities, or behave irrationally in sexual situations to minimize or dismiss their anxieties and worries.

- **Panic Disorder**

Panic disorder first appears in adolescence, typically between the ages of fifteen and nineteen, and is more common in girls than in boys. Intense panic can strike for no apparent reason, or certain circumstances might bring it on, referred to as a panic attack.

A child experiencing a panic attack could experience overwhelming anxiety or discomfort, a sense of impending doom, the worry that he's losing his mind, or surreal feelings. Shortness of breath, sweating, coughing, chest pains, nausea, disorientation, and numbness or tingling in his extremities may accompany the emotional symptoms. Some teenagers may experience a sense of impending death or lose their ability to reason during an attack. Many young people who suffer panic attacks worry that they may experience more episodes and strive to stay away from situations that they think might bring them on. The teens can start to avoid routine activities and routines due to this frightened anticipation.

- **Phobias**

Many fears experienced by younger children are minor, transient, and thought normal for their development stage. Some teenagers experience phobias, which are irrational, frequently unfounded anxieties focused on certain things or circumstances. These severe anxieties may restrict a teen's activities. A phobia causes excessive fear that is not a sensible reaction to the environment.

With age, a child's phobia triggers frequently evolve. Extremely young children may fear the dark, monsters, or real hazards, whereas adolescents' phobic anxieties usually revolve around school and social performance.

Numerous studies have shown a rise in middle or junior high school dropout rates. With school avoidance, persistent concerns about academic achievement or peer pressure may cause the unwillingness to attend classes regularly. Anxiety, bodily issues, and school avoidance follow as a result of this. The cycle intensifies as physical problems like headaches, migraines, and menstruation cramps worsen. Usually, doctor's visits don't reveal any general medical causes. The longer a teen skips school, the more difficult it is for him to overcome his anxiety and fear and return to school. He feels increasingly alienated from extracurricular activities at school unlike other kids.

Some children are more reserved by nature than others, and as they go through puberty, when their bodies, voices, and emotions change, they could become even more self-conscious. Even though they may feel unsure initially, most teenagers can participate if given time to observe and warm up. In severe cases, known as social phobia, the adolescent withdraws greatly and finds it difficult to overcome his profound self-doubt and anxiety to engage in social activities. The adolescent with social phobia gets enslaved to unwavering anxieties of other people's judgment or expectations when confronted with entering a new or unfamiliar social scenario. He might worry about his well-being, appearance, or general competency as a way to cope with his social awkwardness. Alternatively, he can exhibit clownish or noisy behavior or turn to drink to ease his nervousness.

Social phobia may coincide with school dropout and be difficult to separate from because the school environment heavily influences a teenager's social life. When a teen with social anxiety avoids attending school, their educational and classroom performance suffers, and their participation in social and recreational activities decreases. As a result, their self-esteem also suffers.

Some teenagers may feel so anxious that they cannot leave the house. Instead of being a dread of the outside world, agoraphobia appears to be a result of feelings about being separated from one's parents and anxieties about leaving home. Several kids who exhibit extreme separation anxiety as toddlers go on to have agoraphobia as teenagers and adults.

- **Causations and Effects**

The majority of scientists think that timidity and anxiousness are inborn tendencies. There is a good probability that if one parent has anxiety tendencies naturally, so will their child. Additionally, a parent's unease is frequently expressed to their child, exacerbating their innate sensitivity. Then, a cycle of growing unease can be created. This child's typical style of experiencing and relating to his world by the time he enters puberty is colored with anxiety. According to certain studies, kids who become anxious or disturbed easily have never learnt how to calm themselves as babies.

Adolescent anxiety disorders frequently have a history of separation anxiety, which is the propensity to experience overwhelming terror if one is removed from one's home or close loved ones, typically a parent. Separation issues can also affect adolescents. Although these teenagers may deny it, separation anxiety may be evident in their aversion to leaving home and being persuaded to engage in the autonomous activity. Teenagers' refusal to enroll in or persist in school is frequently caused by separation anxiety.

Avoiding school might occur after a big shift at school, like entering middle school or junior high. It might also be brought on by anything unrelated to school, including a death in the family, a divorce, or an illness. Some children develop fears related to gang activity or a lack of safety at school.

Anxious teenagers are less successful in academics, athletics, and interpersonal connections. An overly anxious teenager may also fall short of his potential. Teens with high anxiety levels may exhibit excessive conformity, perfectionism, and self-doubt. He might redo chores or put off doing them to win approval or avoid receiving them. A worried young person frequently seeks excessive reassurance about who he is and whether he is good enough.

Teenagers with anxiety problems can also struggle with eating disorders or mood issues. Teenagers with ongoing anxiety may also experience suicidal thoughts or act self-destructively; in these cases, help is needed immediately. Teens who experience anxiety may also turn to substances like alcohol and narcotics for self-medication, self-soothing, or ritual development.

- **How to React**

If your adolescent is willing to discuss his worries and fears, pay close attention and treat him respectfully. Help him understand that growing feelings of uncertainty about his body, performance, peer acceptance, and overall security are all normal aspects of puberty without downplaying his sentiments.

You might be able to assist him in lessening the overpowering magnitude of his sentiments by assisting him in tracing his anxiousness to particular situations and experiences. Assure him that while his worries are valid, he will probably be able to manage them and that as he ages, he will learn new coping mechanisms to deal with stress and worry.

Remind him of past occasions when he first felt anxious but overcame it to engage in novel circumstances, like junior high school or camp. Despite his reluctance, acknowledge him when he participates. Express your pride in his capacity to act despite feeling a great deal of fear. Remember that your teen may not always feel comfortable discussing emotions that he perceives as indicators of weakness. Even if it may appear that he is not listening right now, your efforts to assist him may subsequently calm him.

Consult a specialist if your teen's anxiety lasts longer than six months or if it starts to dominate his life and restrict his activities. A child and adolescent psychiatrist or another specialist in treating teenagers can be suggested by his doctor or teacher.

As with any teenage emotional disturbance, managing anxiety disorders requires a combination of therapy measures. The best strategy must be tailored to the adolescent and his family. Although these illnesses can significantly disturb and disrupt the teen's life, the prognosis is often positive.

An assessment of symptoms, the teen's family and social background, and the degree of interference or impairment is the first step in treating an anxiety problem. Both the teenager's parents and themselves should be included in this process. School personnel and records may be contacted to determine how the disease has affected the teen's performance and function in school.

The evaluator will also consider any underlying physical conditions or disorders, such as diabetes, that may contribute to anxiety symptoms. A study of medications that could make people anxious, such as some asthma medications, will take place. A doctor may also consider the young person's diet because excessive levels of caffeine, such as those found in coffee or soft drinks, might create agitation. We will also consider any additional biological, psychological, familial, or societal factors that may put the child at risk for excessive anxiety.

A clinician will look into other possibilities before classifying a teen's refusal to attend school as school avoidance. It's possible that the adolescent is experiencing harassment or threats, is sad, or has an undiagnosed learning problem. He might not be skipping class out of concern for his performance or separation from his buddies but rather to spend time with them.

Suppose the adolescent has acted in a suicidal or self-destructive manner, tried to self-medicate with drink or drugs, or is gravely depressed. In that case, these issues need to be addressed immediately. Hospitalization may be advised in these situations to safeguard the child.

Most of the time, treating anxiety disorders involves limiting its negative impacts on the teen's social, academic, and developmental advancement, diminishing its symptoms, and alleviating its discomfort. The initial objective will be to get the young person back to school as quickly as possible if the issue shows up as school avoidance.

o **Behavioral Cognitive Therapy**

Techniques used in cognitive-behavioral therapy frequently treat teenage anxiety issues successfully. These methods assist the adolescent in examining his anxiety, identifying situations when it is likely to occur, and comprehending its implications. This can assist a child in recognizing the exaggerated nature of his anxieties and formulating a solution. The teen participates actively in cognitive-behavioral treatment, which tends to be relevant to the anxiety problem and usually deepens the young person's knowledge. Below are some tips for parents.

Tip 1: Address Their Anxiety Appropriately.

Even though it might seem apparent, it's crucial for parents of worried kids to keep their calm and be upbeat as much as they can. How you react to your child's thoughts and behaviors can have a significant impact on how adaptable they are.

Talk to your youngster about their fears.

To start a discussion, ask your youngster to share their feelings about their fears. Telling a child not to worry or to stop reflecting on their problems is neither motivating nor validating. It is best to tell your child that experiencing fear is natural and to emphasize that you will always be there for them.

If your child has problems verbally expressing themselves, encourage them to do so by telling a story. By going outside, your child may feel more comfortable and be more capable of expressing their emotions.

Show Concern and Understanding.

Collaboration while demonstrating support and empathy can be a powerful strategy for coming up with workable solutions. Research shows that mothers' empathy much helps to lessen children's distress.

Inform your child that feeling anxious is natural and that you are willing to assist them pinpoint the source of their anxiety and develop coping techniques. Together, you and your child can strengthen your relationship and teach each other how to deal with anxiety.

Be Motivating Rather Than Authoritative.

The idea is to help your child manage their anxiety without becoming overly protective in an effort to make it go away. By being attentive and empathetic, you are already doing a lot to help.

Additionally, you can talk about various strategies for handling particular situations. If your child, for example, has separation anxiety and is terrified to go home after visiting a friend, think about appropriate alternatives. For instance, your child could ask the friend's parents to call you to find out what time you'll be taking them away. These kinds of strategies can calm your child and reduce their anxiety.

Develop Your Child's Coping Skills.

Instead of attempting to prevent your child's anxiety sources, you might help them develop effective coping skills. Regularly praising your youngster will make them feel better capable and confident. Establish modest yet manageable goals. Every time a goal is achieved, you may add, "I'm very proud of how you handled the issue and worked over your anxiety."

If your child exhibits any resilience or faces their fears, commend them for their work. Assure your child that a setback is not a failure but rather a teaching moment that will help them overcome obstacles in the future. Talk to them about what they could do properly the following time to get better results. They'll feel more in control as they exercise their authority.

Tip 2: Lead by Example.

Your kid needs your assistance in learning how to cope with stress and concern because they try looking up to you. A good illustration is how you express your rage and irritation. Keep as much tolerance and composure as you can when coping with problems and tough situations. The way you talk and engage in conversations can have a big impact on even a tough teenager's values and behavior.

Parents who take care of themselves by getting adequate sleep, exercising regularly, and eating a healthy diet might encourage their children to do the same. If you practice relaxing techniques like yoga, mindfulness, or other types of breathing, your children may grow to be more self-aware. But don't criticize your physique because doing so could lead to body shaming and a poor self-image.

If you maintain a healthy lifestyle, your kids can learn valuable lessons from you. We all make errors, and children should learn that despite their parents' flaws, they are still capable of overcoming obstacles. This can help by removing unnecessary demands that might make your youngster more uneasy.

Tip 3: Teach Your Child How to Relax.

Invite your child to join you in some mindfulness or exercises in deep breathing. This will enable you to understand how they are feeling and suggest proactive relaxing practices that you can both try. Children often have breathlessness when they are anxious. Try having your child relax deeply while placing one palm on their heart while the other is on their belly. When they breathe in and out, their bellies should expand and contract respectively.

The two elements of mindful breathing are concentrating on breathing and giving attention to the present moment. Request that your child close their eyes and take a few deep breaths. When they inhale, they could check for tight areas on their body. The irritation in these places can then be imagined to be replaced by a warm, comfortable feeling.

With older children and teenagers, examine various yoga styles, meditation techniques, mental imagery, and other relaxation techniques.

Switching off mobile and social media gadgets and entering one's "happy spot" is a useful habit to put into regular practice. Your teen can think of a specific event or memory that gives them a sense of safety, comfort, and contentment. Maybe this has something to do with lying on the beach, going to a peaceful place, or being in the heart of nature. The greatest method to enter this relaxed state is to visualize beautiful scenes or soothing sounds.

Tip 4: Encourage Healthy Sleep Habits.

Developing a predictable and comforting sleep plan is essential since worried children sometimes struggle to fall asleep. Establish a consistent sleep schedule, avoid caffeine, and cut back on exercise and exposure to light in the hours before bed.

When it's time to go to bed, make sure your child is at comfortable and secure with few interruptions to promote sleep. Their bedroom should be welcoming, calm, and cool. Screen usage on laptops, smartphones, TVs, or computer games should be kept to a minimum at least an hour before bedtime. You should read to your youngster or put on some calming music at this time. If there is a fluorescent bulb, or if a young child has a stuffed animal or nice blanket to hug, they may feel safer.

Tip 5: Promote Responsible Social Media Usage

Since studies have demonstrated both positive and bad effects, it is a good idea to start by discussing the advantages and disadvantages of social media with children. You can take the following more effective measures rather than merely pleading with your child to put their device away, which may only make them feel more anxious:

1. Setting a positive example for your child by limiting your use of social media and screens will benefit you both.
2. Urge your child to participate in more creative pursuits, talk with friends in reality, and participate in more social interaction rather than focused on how many "likes" their posts on social media earn. If young children are not exposed to screens, they will learn other ways to entertain themselves.
3. Establish a set time when no one in the family is allowed to use their phones or laptops. This can be completed as a quick daily task or over the weekend while you're occupied with family outings.
4. Remind them that photos on social media are often digitally manipulated and do not truly represent reality. The amount of enjoyment was regularly exaggerated in posts about events or gatherings to which they were not invited.
5. Instruct your child to exercise caution when posting comments about others and to stay away from those who criticize them online. Particularly among teenagers, impulsivity and ignorance of the possible harm or outrageousness of the content shared are risk factors.

Limit your child's screen usage if social media interferes with their ability to learn, sleep, or participate in extracurricular activities.

THE END NOTE

Anxiety might seem like an invasive mind grabber that takes too much time squeezing, startling, and overwhelming everyone it comes in contact with due to the rapid changes that come along with puberty. Any person may find it challenging to cope with anxiety. The great news is that if anxiety becomes a danger, there are methods to lower it to a bearable level. Understanding the warning signs of anxiety and their causes is essential before that. By realizing this, anxiety will start to lose some of its enigmatic and erratic power.

Hey Teens: You should be sure to show yourself more love. The world is starting to become more accessible to you as you enter adolescence. Your wisdom, bravery, and interesting and highly admirable point of view are what the world really needs. Despite the inclination of anxiety to focus all too frequently on the negative aspects of ourselves, the features in ourselves that we wish to change the most in the majority of the time have some very amazing strengths packed into them. Despite the fact that you would always like to be anxiety-free, you have several advantages. Spend some time watching them.

You are not anxious; anxiety is something that happens. You are a reliable person who has ideas no one else has thought of and are imaginative, sensitive, courageous, and strong. Along with being extremely intelligent and emotionally intelligent, you also have a fantastic and original way of seeing things. Because of your personality, most people would choose you. Simply implement the ideas that are emphasized in this book. Work on improving yourself, use these worksheets and exercises, and lead a healthy lifestyle.

Printed in Great Britain
by Amazon